The Gateway of Liberation
and
Spiritual Laws

Blessings to you,

Carol E. Parrish

Books by Mary Gray

The Gateway of Liberation
The Temple of Amon Ra
Echoes of the Cosmic Song
Heavenly Choristers
The Chalice of the Heart

Books by Carol E. Parrish-Harra

The Book of Rituals
Personal and Planetary Transformation

The Aquarian Rosary
Reviving the Art of Mantra Yoga

The New Age Handbook on Death and Dying

Messengers of Hope

(in addition to numerous teaching tapes)

THE GATEWAY OF LIBERATION
and
SPIRITUAL LAWS:
RULES OF THE EVOLUTIONARY ARC

This Expanded Third Edition contains an introduction,
biographical vignette of Mary Gray and glossary by
Carol E. Parrish-Harra, Ph.D.

PRINTED IN THE UNITED STATES OF AMERICA BY
SPARROW HAWK PRESS

SPARROW HAWK VILLAGE
22 SUMMIT RIDGE DRIVE
TAHLEQUAH, OKLAHOMA 74464

Grateful acknowledgment is given to the Agni Yoga Society and Nicholas
Roerich Museum, New York City, for their permission to reprint the
copyrighted excerpt from *Leaves of Morya's Garden, Vol. II*, by Helena
Roerich, 1925, ©1952, used in the Dedication.

99 98 97 96 95 94 93 92   5 4 3 2 1

Expanded by Carol E. Parrish-Harra, Ph.D.
Book design and editing by Mary Beth Marvin

Special thanks to the group who helped to make this book possible, including
Karen Dillinger, administrative coordination, John R. Eggen, Jr., marketing
management, Gerald Mobley, cover art and graphics, Eliot Ricciardelli,
project management, Richard A. Smith, marketing design and Stephen
Tiesman, typesetting.

Library of Congress Cataloging-in-Publication Data
Gray, Mary
The Gateway of Liberation
and
Spiritual Laws
Including biographical vignette, introductions and glossary by Carol E.
Parrish-Harra.   1. Universal law 2. Religion 3. Evolution
Library of Congress Catalog Card Number 91-068495
ISBN 0-945027-06-0

TO THE SONS OF FIRE IN ALL WORLDS

Time was when We said: "Give up everything."
Now We go further and say: "Take everything but
do not consider it your own."

Leaves of Morya's Garden, Vol. II

Editor's Note: Mary Gray's writing style, gender use and punctuation were quite correct in 1935. Modernization of this revised edition was directed primarily toward punctuation to prevent distraction. In order to maintain the integrity and the historic value of this publication, only minimal changes in the original writing were made. —mbm

CONTENTS

A Biographical Vignette of Mary Gray
by Carol E. Parrish-Harra

The work of Mary (Mrs. Roland) Gray came to my attention years ago when I discovered *The Gateway of Liberation* for the first time. Something in me embraced the lady and took her to my heart. She is one of the more silent ones whom most of us interested in mysticism in this modern day do not know. But **I believe her work helped to pave our path.**

Born in Paris, France, she was the daughter of an artist, William Tudor of Boston, Massachusetts. Mary was educated at Bryn Mawr and Radcliffe. Among her family's close friends were Ralph Waldo Emerson, William James, Julia Ward Howe, Col. Higginson and others of the group of liberal minds of New England.

Early in her life she basked in such philosophic thought, and she grew to contemplate the serious side of life. She remained a student of mysticism and knew personally many of the outstanding leaders of philosophy in both the United States and Europe. With a variety of interests, she was a compelling speaker — on both sides of the water, both publicly and on the radio. She concerned herself with international issues, as well as the enlightenment of individuals.

The mother of several children, Mary Gray was deeply interested in education. She established two schools, successively, in California which operated for some years, devoted to her conviction that character building formed the basis of civilization.

A frequent speaker on oriental philosophy and Christian mysticism, she wrote five books, building bridges of understanding in such areas as inner and outer life, the question of good and evil, spiritual law, as well as a captivating Egyptian story of the Temple of Heliopolis as the Age of Darkness descended.

Although Egypt was well known for its high civilization and its advanced period, Mary Gray wrote of its little-contemplated fall. She acknowledged the pain of the corruption of sacred teachings and the struggle that ensued.

As the time is rapidly approaching for the reemergence of the mysteries, we enjoy again the penetrating thoughts of Mary Gray as she creates bridges in our minds, leading us from the outer to the inner as we grasp the thoughts that reconcile.

Mary Gray authored *The Gateway of Liberation, America — the Cradle of the New Race, Echoes of the Cosmic Song, The Temple of Amon Ra, Heavenly Choristers, The Chalice of the Heart* and *Spiritual Laws — Rules of the Evolutionary Arc.*

Please contemplate *The Gateway of Liberation* and *Spiritual Laws.* The wisdom of Mary Gray accords a guide to cosmic thought.

FOREWORD
by Mary Gray

There come into incarnation in various countries certain souls who have reached a point in evolution where they turn their faces steadfastly from the world toward that Mountain of Light which some call God.

In the resources of worldly pleasure, of human happiness, of knowledge or of power they find no comfort. They are goaded by the sense of being trapped in a world which offers them no satisfying purpose for living, no food for the soul.

They see that happiness here endures not, power fails, pleasure palls, and they are filled, therefore, with unceasing restlessness of mind and spirit. With constant reiteration the great questions, *why,* and *to what end,* arise in their souls.

It is for such that what follows is written. It is for those who know that personal happiness passes and that power but rouses hatred. These pages are offered for those who desire earnestly to know the purpose of life, the reason for man's existence upon this planet, something of the plan and the way of fulfillment. Those who are still content with their daily round of duties, pleasures, services as yet need no further aid.

But upon the many crossroads of our planet — its byways and highways — travel those who seek the Gateway of Liberation at the end of the Path of Initiation. In some long-past time the seed of occult truth was planted in their hearts, a vision of the gateway which leads to the shining land of Brotherhood casts a light upon their souls which urged them life after life to seek the reality which lay behind the vision.

Perchance some wise teacher gave them knowledge of the Pearl of pearls and led their still human feet to the entrance of that way which leads to divinity. And now today there rises again within the imperative need to storm the rocky heights which guard the citadel which, when attained, makes man no longer son of man, but Son of God.

That the way may be a little clearer, that the search may be a little more eager, that the realities may shine more clearly, these pages are inscribed.

Above and beyond all things, if the Path is to be found and if the Path is to be trod, the vision of the goal, like a lodestar, must rouse in the soul that holy fire which alone can give the power to achieve.

Introduction to *The Gateway of Liberation*
by Carol E. Parrish-Harra

Modern life is so full and rich — every desire seems to be attainable. Some enjoy the passion for gain, for power and pursuit; yet the one of simple heart often pines for an intangible something more. Neither work nor play fulfills. Sweet pleasure too soon loses its savor. The seeker weeps for the unknown, wipes the tears and laments the sensitive nature that seems to turn away from the world's offerings. This heart — modern and vital, tender and clear — finds no lasting joy in what life has to offer.

The aspirant who has heard the echo of the cosmic song suffers. In sleep this one has tasted the elixir of the gods. Where are mind and knowing when one so desires the sweet food of paradise? One only knows disquiet; conscious mind is no ally; discontent mounts. Friends comfort for brief moments as the soul within comes to life — like a foot asleep, tingling with unwarranted pain.

The outer world holds little charm; the inner world is like a fragrance — wafting, clear for an instant, and lost again. The physical body either houses the soul or lures it from its world. Somehow one knows the challenge — yet can see it not; embraces life — yet loves it not; seeks the greater Life — yet is unable to find the entryway. One stands happy and sad, reflecting on the stream of light that shines through the ethers, **knowing** this narrow path of shimmering moonlight has something to offer — yet perceives not what.

Now, dear one, it is time to know. Dare to step upon that path and walk to the Source of Life. Angry voices may cry out, "Step not there, it is not for you." Lonely voices might beg, "Seek me instead." But the heart knows the soul must depart and walk the path that only those who are ready can tread. With courage draped about one's shoulders, the sword of discrimination fixed at one's side, the mind submits itself to training when the heart is no longer seduced by the outer world.

Not one more step without the inner will I go — for here I walk, knowing each step may be a trap and each reward false. Mists of glamour float lightly; illusion reigns. Every hope swells to taunt when I approach the door that leads *no-where*. The No-Thing dwells here in the mists of forgotten life. A single, focused note reverberates in the senses — but its echo can be heard from time to time. The soul knows what it must do.

Enter now upon the stream of moonlight. The brilliant light of day is the goal of the child of knowing; the soft moonlight prepares one to remember and relax into the hidden ways of training, that all who discover the mystery teachings may in time come to the light of high consciousness. Out of sight, moonlight nurtures the ancient memory of a life forgotten and of the secrets whispered to the infant soul when it left its home to dwell among those who had donned the cloak of form.

Remember: to walk in the Light is to energize the soul — that it may have eyes and ears, that it may find its way into the gossamer land of heaven and bring to Earth its inner knowing.

Enter here, O one who would. Enter this mysterious land, and weave the mind that is ready to Know, to Do and to Be.

Remember the note sung long ago, imprinted on the ethers of the soul. Hear the sound of the Master's voice, O one most hungry. When the eyes can cry no more and the line between pleasure and pain is lost, enter here — through the gateway of liberation.

PART I
The Path of Probation

CHAPTER 1
The Awakening

In order that man might sooner break through the thrall of passing pleasures and hearken to the laws of evolution, the great Teachers have again and again spoken the Truth, that life of itself is plain and that no lasting happiness may here be found.

If one really grasps this fact and ceases to follow the will-o'-the-wisp, ever elusive of personal happiness, the mind lies open to receive the Truth: the purpose of life as seen from the consciousness of the Infinite. This Truth is visioned by the seers from age to age for man's guidance when he feels the need arise for light upon his path.

When the hour comes in which a human soul truly recognizes its bondage and longs for freedom, then does the mind open to receive the light heretofore shut away by the constant search for Earthly happiness.

Some do not reach this point until the period of possible Earthly happiness passes and old age approaches. Then, as they look back upon their lives and upon the past, they wonder what has been gained by this succession of generations, each spending its life caring for and preparing for the next, century after century.

Nations rise and fall. The progress of civilization is uncertain and unstable. A cataclysm comes — war, disaster, earthquake — and the fruits of many years, of many lives, of many nations are swept away. What is the value of this human struggle? What then is the purpose — what the law?

When man awakens to a need for a knowledge of the law, when the mind is thus open, then may be given the true understanding of evolution and the final purpose of human incarnation.

It is a high purpose — the gaining of mind — the achievement of independent judgment through the knowledge of good and evil.

This gained gives to man the power of creative thought, the power of Kriyashakti (the power of divine Creation), of forming universes, various in kind, method and evolution.

This is the power that the devas or angels have not — and until they gain it they are the servants of those who have it.

The Holy Spirit — Mahat — alone has the power to create, and it is the creative function upon the physical plane which is the gift of the Holy Spirit and promise of the future creative power on every plane as man learns the secret of the control and the use of sex, speech and thought.

This unfoldment of creative power under the Third Logos comes only as a sequence to the unfoldment of the powers of Will and Wisdom under the First and Second Logoi which has been done in past systems. It is the critical period of evolution when man ventures his eternal life to win "salvation," the mastery of his own spirit, awakening the Godhood within him.

To gain his heritage of conscious divinity and the divine attributes of creative power which follow upon this, he must be immersed in matter, cut away from the inner wisdom, from spiritual light and from his consciousness of God, that he may unfold vision, light and the Godhead within himself. He must meet evil — which is but the other pole of good, negative and positive, attraction and repulsion — in order that he may know it, may control it and so may use it.

For evil, so-called, is involution, a necessary part of all cosmic development in the earlier stages, associated with the descent into matter, the assimilation of form. That which we know as evil is evil only on the evolutionary arc when man is rising out of matter to his Source, to unveil the God-Within. The evolutionary forces represent evil on the involutionary arc, just as the involutionary forces represent evil on the evolutionary arc. Evil is that which is a hindrance to achieving the purposes of the soul at any given point of development.

We must vision man's career as an arc of descent and ascent. During the descent into matter he is veiling himself in denser and denser form in which the God is hidden; he is building a form — more and more selfish and self-centred, more and more powerful, more and more separate — in which he may enclose the Divine Flame that it may gain isolation. Only thus separated and thus detached at once from its Source, the Universal Godhead, and from its fellows can it gain conscious, separate, individual Divinity.

Therefore, on the descending or involutionary arc the law of man must be selfishness, isolation, combat, until the form is vigorous and dense enough an animal to safeguard his isolation and to hide effectually his divinity. This is the period of the savage or of the animal which is governed by the law of the survival of the fittest that the bodies may become powerful.

This accomplished, man is given his heritage of mind — the spark of divine ideation, logic, reason. As he slowly evolves mind, he evolves the power which shall give him control ultimately of the creative forces of the universe and of himself, as mirroring the Macrocosm in the Microcosm, as reflecting God in man.

The law of the evolutionary arc — when man seeks to use the animal he has built to manifest his divine powers, when he seeks to become the mirror of God — must be the law of sacrifice and unselfishness.

During the unfoldment of mind, surrounded by all forces, both good and evil, man's path is difficult. He knows not good from evil and manifests both.

The test of his insight will come in his choice. It will be proved if he can choose the evolutionary forces which will carry him upward to his divinity. If he embraces the involutionary forces, he endangers his heritage, and at the time of ultimate choice he may choose destruction, not salvation and Godhead.

Manas, the higher mind, of itself gives knowledge, insight, independent creative power. Gaining the powers of mind is the purpose of our present evolution.

It is a long and arduous task lasting through many aeons as man, driven by desire, checked by pain, goaded by necessity, slowly awakens from his mental lethargy, from his heedless response to impulse.

At last, to escape painful conditions about him or to attain his desires, he begins to use his intelligence. Man in his early development is by nature lazy, both physically and mentally, and shrinks from protracted thought or from the continued action required by a plan, mind-born, which must be carried out.

He must, therefore, in the earlier days constantly be driven by three goads: fear, pain and hatred. These are aroused in him by the conflict in the world; by the cruelty of his conditions; by hunger, sickness, loss, want, cold and all other human ills.

Only such goads will drive inert minds into the processes of sustained thought. And as sustained thought alone can unfold the powers of the mind, we find these goads throughout much of the earlier stages of human life. All institutions which tend to relieve man from the necessity of thought or to repress in him independent thought are against evolution.

In the beginning of the development of mind, it is not important how a man thinks or what causes him to think. The one essential is to develop the faculty of thought; and as the savage man is too underdeveloped to respond to the higher motives of ambition, desire for achievement, spiritual aspiration or unselfish love, he must be reached by the only spurs that he can recognize.

As the greatest virtues the race knows — power, compassion and knowledge — spring lotus-like from the roots of wrath, lust and greed, so the unfoldment of the divine quality of mind is spurred in its beginning by fear and hatred and pain.

As man evolves, the goads of fear and hate are replaced by others more suited to the evolving spirit. But throughout evolution on the physical plane, pain remains as the great friend and teacher of man, refining the bodies, uplifting the soul, guarding him from error and from false paths and leading him by slow steps to the heights of self-sacrifice which shall at last make him divine.

Yet, withal, since the greatest danger ultimately to the race lies in the unfoldment of mind not dominated by the softening influences of compassion and spiritual wisdom — buddhi — throughout the ages come the spiritual teachers to voice the law of love, of spiritual aspiration, of man's divinity and of his responsibility for his brother man.

In his ruthless struggle, only as he remembers the need for love can he safely unfold the latent powers of mind, insulated and protected by buddhi, from becoming destructive. It is within a sheath of love that manas must unfold.

To keep the sheath of love active, to rouse in man the principles which will permit him to gain knowledge tinctured by wisdom, the brain guarded and controlled by the heart is the work of the spiritual messengers. They teach of man's mission, of his divine origin and of his future heritage. They mark the path in the wilderness of worldly life which will lead out of chaos into attainment and peace.

Lest man, blind and cut away in the turmoil of mind building, lose all memory or understanding of his real mission, the teachers come; lest man be enmeshed by the things of the world — passion and power — they come to hold before him the vision of the goal. Ultimately he must achieve his Godhood, having gained by this arduous journey the jewel of mind. This will put him higher than the angels, not only servant to the law — as the angels who have not yet achieved the power of creative mind still must be — but Master of the Law.

There lies in evolution a nicely adjusted balance: mind to be gained but not at the cost of spiritual salvation. Is it any marvel that many are lost on the way, that they lose the vision of eternal things in the muck and mire of the fight and learn to struggle for themselves alone, forgetful of their divine nature and of the law of sacrifice and of compassion by which they must at last evolve!

Guarded by impersonal love, the mind can attain divinity and its divine heritage of power. Unless it works within the matrix of buddhi, unless it unfolds within the sheath of unifying love, its intense, separate and destructive activity may tear it away from its higher principles and leave it an isolated unit, robbed of its hope of salvation on this planet.

As said before, throughout the ages spiritual teachers come to stimulate activity — first, of those planes of emotion, or kama, which are directly linked with compassion or buddhi, and second, through these, of buddhi itself. Until true universal compassion, buddhi, can become active, the sheathing of astral love must enfold the mind.

Therefore, one finds marriage required in the older religions. Through marriage man learns love and personal attachment, and he learns to temper the destructiveness of mind for those he loves and for all dependent things. Marriage is a necessity to evolving man until tenderness is strongly established.

This shows clearly the place of woman in the earlier parts of the scheme. Polarized in kama — emotion and desire — she constantly stimulates emotion in man and through that a reflection in buddhi or impersonal love. She is the agent of love during all the earlier cycles — expressing not mind but feeling, always holding the ideal of the home, of tenderness, of children balanced against man's desire for power and conquest.

She is the brake upon the wheel of his progress which guards him from himself, which guards him from developing too far the single equality of mind. She reflects for the world the ideal of compassion, of love, of tenderness. Her compassion is often unjust and unwise, but man's justice is often equally unrighteous, seen from the inner vision. It is through the reacting of these mutually irreconcilable forces that the world is safeguarded from manas — mind.

Passion and chivalry are so engrafted in the man as to render him susceptible to woman's influence. The fact that this susceptibility is often used to betray him does not alter the necessity for its existence for it is the portal to his fortress — the granite citadel of mind — by which may enter that love and tenderness which alone can save him from himself.

As years progress and the cycle turns, man will reach a point where increasing tenderness expresses itself in him, and at that time passion will lose its hold, its purpose fulfilled. Then woman, attaining greater powers of mind but of an intuitive and abstract type, will complement him on each plane equally — not as now, on alternate planes.

At present man is strongly polarized in the physical and mental more than in the emotional and intuitional as is woman, and thus they supplement one another. In time men and women will develop aspects complementary to one another on all planes, thus becoming far more useful to one another in the work of the world.

The work of the Lords of Compassion has been touched upon before. They send out messengers of light to soften the hardness of men's hearts and to keep ever before them in the turmoil which is unfolding mind the underlying law of unity, of love. When the conflict becomes too bitter, then come the messengers again to open the path of love.

This they do, first, to keep the balance of forces. Men must not lose sight of the ultimate goal. Thus will they be protected from falling into the dangers of the extremes of mental arrogance.

Secondly, they come to mark the Path for those who are ready to step out of human evolution into superhuman, to begin to climb the seven steps which lead to divinity. A point comes in evolution when individual men have attained the necessary development of mind and may graduate from the turmoil and trouble of this world to become "pillars of God who shall go out no more."

They become, then, conscious cooperators and agents for God in carrying out His plans in our world. For these men the Path of Liberation must be clearly defined, for they become the disciples of the teachers, following in their footsteps the law of love, of renunciation and of self-conquest.

Thus, we see every great teacher surrounded by a few to whom he teaches the Way of Liberation, the steps which lead to the final unfoldment of spiritual potency. It is they who become the saints of each religion and who carry on the tradition of the Path of Liberation and of Light to future generations.

To those who search deep in the secret annals of any great religion will appear mention or traces of the teaching which bear upon this Path. In every age, however, of those who seek the Path of Initiation, but few shall find it and fewer shall tread it to the end.

But the Path remains ever in existence, and the way may be found by those who bend the energies of their souls to the task. In ancient parlance it was sometimes called the Philosopher's Stone and those who found it spoke not of it to others.

Today the stress of the world is so great that many souls are ceasing to hope that happiness may be found in the experiences of human life. They are ready, therefore, for the reception of the word of man's purpose in evolution and of the Way to Liberation. For these the qualifications for discipleship are being spoken and the way of attainment thereof unfolded.

CHAPTER 2
The Requirements for Discipleship

The requirements for discipleship are:
1. Recognition of the purpose of life
2. Balancing the karmic debt
3. Orientation to the Path
4. Study of the character, weighing it
5. Awakening compassion to balance mind

The first requirement for discipleship is the recognition of the true conditions of worldly life and the determination to seek something better, to use life here as a stepping-stone to spiritual achievement. This is called the awakening, and until this takes place there is no hope of treading the Path.

The mind must definitely turn away from the hope of personal happiness here and seek the Path. In passing, one should say that the renunciation of Earthly happiness does not destroy it. On the contrary, usually it brings happiness as a result of the work of the Path, for true happiness comes not from gratified desire but from love and service for others.

Personal happiness passes. The ones we love die, betray us or leave us, and our solitary way leads but to the grave. Such fragments of personal happiness vouchsafed to us are but divine reflections of that universal joy and peace which pulses at the heart of Being. As we teach our personalities here to become instruments of the God-Within, as we learn to give our love and compassion to a sorrowing world, asking no return, we bring ourselves in touch with this universal joy which pours ever more strongly through us as we keep the channels open through love and sacrifice.

The motive of human life must no longer be the search for happiness but the quest for truth. In this exploration sooner or later the disciple is stripped of all things he holds most dear. In after-days these may be given again to him but only after he has shown that he can go on without them and that they can never bind him.

The pilgrim must journey alone, lightly laden. On the Path he may find companions to cheer his way, but he may not turn aside to dally with them nor leave the Path to succor them if they fall away.

When the disciple sees the world as it is and definitely turns away from it, this is called the *awakening,* the first step in discipleship.

The second is the beginning of balancing the karmic sheet. He must study the conditions in which he finds himself, determining as clearly as possible what debts he owes and what bonds must be broken. He sets himself to making no new bonds and to equalizing the debts as soon as possible, incurring no new ones that he may be free for work.

To achieve a clear view of his conditions, his mind must be dispassionate, calm, aloof, and he must see himself not as a worldly entity surrounded by people and conditions to whom he owes worldly duties but as a divine spirit come into the world of causes and effects to achieve certain divine purposes of its own.

All things which interfere with the achievement of this purpose must be put aside. Such debts as he feels unavoidable he must pay as rapidly as possible and realize the payment must be determined not by the desires and opinions of his friends and family but by the vision of the divine spirit within him, conscious at last of its mission.

It should be remembered that those who seek to interfere with the fulfillment of this mission create bad karma; often the disciple, for the sake of those he loves, must not permit them to lay bonds upon him. Nor must he hesitate for one moment as to where his allegiance lies. It can be only to the God-Within.

Before that transcendent claim, all lesser claims fall away. "He that loveth father or mother more than Me is not worthy of Me." Here the Christ spoke not for Himself but voiced the cry of that divine spirit within each man of which He was the expression, that Universal Spirit linked to each human vehicle which sends Its messengers to sound Its call for obedience and allegiance.

When the balance sheet of karmic debt has been drawn and the man has oriented himself truly and steadfastly to the goal, he sweeps away within himself all desires that can bind: desires for love, for home, for comfort, for companionship — all those desires which every soul, even upon a worldly mission, must put aside, whether to save his nation by war, to aid science by discovery or to seek the Antarctic pole.

There must be no clinging to personal things. He stands free, having taken the spiritual vow of poverty — poverty not in worldly possessions but in the personal treasures of the soul. Henceforth, one goal alone guides the disciple and dominates his actions: seeking the divine within.

This purpose clear, his affairs ordered and organized, the disciple sets himself to achieve powers of mind and heart which shall prepare him for his mighty task. Having envisaged his outer conditions and freed himself mentally and spiritually from outer personal bondage, he now turns his attention to the character which he has built during many aeons. Here too must the balance sheet be made of qualities and defects so that harmony may be achieved in the inner kingdom of the mind and heart as in the outer life.

In the course of many ages of experience, jewels of the spirit have been acquired but overlaid many times with dust and rubbish. This rubbish must be cleared away, the jewels polished and cut. The rubbish consists of prejudices, inaccuracies, intolerances, injustices and personal defects, such as impatience, irritation, disorder, slovenliness. These must be steadfastly absolved, leaving the jewels of courage, accuracy, patience, tolerance, unselfishness, humility and charity.

The mind awakened, the outward conditions analyzed and the debts begun to be paid, inner conditions analyzed and the work launched upon the rounding out of character, there remains the arousing of the spiritual nature. This means awakening compassion for the human race, the recognition of one's essential unity through God with man and responsibility, therefore, to help in man's evolution.

Before one's nature is awakened to the purpose of life and to the nature of the goal, the help vouchsafed to the world is of little value. It is unavailing and useless to help man upon his way when one does not know the direction to travel. Therefore, the first requirement for one who would help is his own awakening. Once he has definitely visioned the purpose and the Path, he finds enough Light to help others upon that Path.

Then must come the recognition that the Path is for all, that the greatest service the disciple renders to man is to tread the Path himself since each step upon that Path leaves it shining more clearly for others! When he finds his foot upon the Path, when he knows himself firmly established and directed to the goal, he may awaken in others the knowledge he has gained. Since ears are deaf when lulled by happiness, only those who have realized the essential pain of human existence can hear. To those he speaks.

When suffering cuts into the heart, when the personal self lies in fragments, many question the wisdom of the Plan, the benevolence of the Powers which bring worlds into manifestation only apparently to suffer and to die. An understanding of the Great Plan alone can restore the sanity of faith. Soon or late, every conscious power, angel or god must pass through the human kingdom to unfold the powers of mind.

Nature in the worlds here below offers much to make the way pleasant, yet the purpose of incarnation is not happiness but the development of mind and of conscious creative power.

In the bitter struggle necessary to attain mind, man is fortunate to have the alleviations he finds in beauty, vigor, companionship and love, for, as said before, the power of mind seems to develop only under the stress of suffering and of the adverse conditions which make up the greater part of human life.

Mind is needful. The greatest danger to man himself, however, is the development of mind unmodified by love, compassion and tenderness — the qualities of divinity. And at this point, where mind is reaching high development among the leaders of the race, it is essential that love and compassion be maintained.

Therefore, today on every side teachers are appearing again preaching the law of love, messengers from the Wise Guardians in the inner worlds who watch over man's progress on the planet. Some messengers are narrow in their view — the white light of eternal truth rayed through a limited brain; some are universal in their touch — witness rising young prophets in so many lands who preach the law of universal brotherhood and international unity.

Yet the purpose behind remains the same — the need of awakening love and compassion in men and in nations that, at this critical period when mind is strong, it shall be guarded by love from destroying the civilization it has built. Man must achieve divinity, but he may only do so through guiding his mind by universal compassion.

CHAPTER 3
Inner Plane Classes

The spiritual progress of the world is not determined only by the messengers who come to speak spiritual truths in this lower world. People are far more responsive to the truth of spiritual things in the inner worlds which they frequent during sleep; and there, night after night, are classes held by those who desire to help awaken men's souls and who teach them while they are out of their bodies in sleep many things which filter through as dim memories or flashes of intuition to the waking consciousness.

Before a man finds in the outer world the light he has been seeking, he has been roused to the search by the things which he has learned on the inner planes.

He has, perhaps, attended one of the great classes or public audiences of Wise Ones of the planet where Their wisdom and radiance are manifest even to the dullest since their spiritual power is not veiled by the gross sheath of mortal flesh and eyes are not dimmed by the ignorance and prejudice of the world below.

The work of these classes is carried on by the Masters Themselves, or by high initiates, in order that Their direct influence may arouse the slumbering spark of spirit within those present.

In the classes in the inner planes are given first the general scheme of evolution and of life, of man's destiny and the method of achievement. When a pupil passes from this class of "hearers" and definitely enrolls himself as a "student," he passes into another group of classes led by chelas, or pupils, for the initial steps of training.

In the outer world he is directed to that literature which embodies the teachings he has been receiving on the inner planes and which he intuitively recognizes, therefore, as true and as that for which he has been searching.

When he proves himself to be in earnest in his desire to tread the Path, the greater part of his teaching thereafter will be in the classes on the inner planes. This teaching will filter through in meditations or in general expansion of consciousness and understanding, especially if he supplements inner work with persistent reading of books which bear upon the Path of Discipleship.

The first class into which the pupil is directed is that which deals with a study of his own vehicles, especially the three lower ones: mind, emotions and body. His training begins with these three. He is taught to consider himself a divine spirit using for contact with the lower worlds three instruments — the instruments of action, feeling and thought.

The first work must be done with mind and thought. Until a man thinks rightly, he cannot wisely undertake training himself. He is taught, therefore, his relation to the inner worlds and to this world in particular, seeing the span of life as a training school in which certain faculties and qualities must be gained.

Each incarnation offers new opportunities to carry on the work unfinished or perhaps marred in the last. If he understands the purpose of incarnation and awakens to his work early in life, much progress can be made. He must know himself as the true arbiter of his own destiny and recognize that the conditions in which he finds himself will never improve unless he makes them improve.

The limitations and bonds which he finds here can be broken but by himself, by his own efforts, by a determination to accept as duties only those which his awakened mind holds as such and to use every available moment of his time in training, study and aspiration.

No human soul is ever wholly free. In every incarnation the necessity for birth, for accepting a family position limits him. Therefore, it is folly to say, "I must wait until I am free." One is never free except as one earns and achieves freedom. A man enters the world bound by associations. Through wise decisions he achieves freedom. This life now is the time to achieve freedom. The power to compel circumstances to yield marks the beginning of growth. Once a man sees that opportunity is now and determines to seize it, he has taken the first step upward. He has oriented his life to the goal.

The Path of Discipleship requires nice decisions. One must act, if possible, with the greatest detachment. At best one sees but a small portion of the Path. When a man has gained a certain measure of discrimination and adjusted his life with the insight it gives him, he turns his attention to the specific control of his vehicles.

The quality of dispassion and desirelessness must be learned, or rather desire to attain the goal must draw all other desires into a single Flame of purpose and will. The pupil is taught to control all lesser desires since they act as bonds upon him. Gradually he must learn indifference to pleasures, permitting nothing to distract him from his major purpose.

This does not mean asceticism or denial of pleasure as wrong, but it means gradual indifference as to whether pleasure comes or not, accepting lightly any happiness that comes but avoiding such pleasures as create desires. All self-indulgence must be overcome.

Even after a man turns his face steadfastly to the goal, strong desires of a noble type often remain — desires for love, for companionship, for association with those we love. Although love in itself is one form of high spirituality, it must not bind; it must pass from intense personal attachment into more intense, impersonal tenderness which can even cause the loved one to suffer if it is in accord with the big plan.

All great achievements are built upon sacrifice, and as a man must put his patriotism to his country before his personal devotion to his wife and family, so a man must put his allegiance to the highest divine law he knows before his personal affections and wishes. It does not mean the sacrifice of the welfare of those one loves. On the contrary those whom we love will profit most by our spiritual achievements for we shall have more to give to them as well as to the world.

But it does mean that all the small obligations and wishes of a personal life must be seen in their true proportion so that jewels of the spirit and high achievements upon the path of divinity may not be thrown lightly aside because of the passing fancies of those who do not understand. Every great achievement the world has ever known has been made possible through sacrifice, sacrifices perhaps unknown and perhaps unrecognized by those close to the one who achieved.

Love must become such that it can bear separation if that too is needed. Of all the requirements this is the hardest. Therefore it is said, "Before the disciple can stand in the presence of the Master, his feet must be washed in the blood of the heart." No man can achieve the goal who does not put the goal, the love of God, above all else.

With this major desire are often minor desires for approval, for appreciation and understanding, for success. Desire for approval in itself is not evil; on the contrary it is good, yet the opinions of others must not swerve the man a hairbreadth from his appointed course nor influence his belief in what is right or wrong for himself.

Lastly come the desires which find expression in the body: the desire for comfort, for luxury, for food of certain types, for beauty. These, too, are bonds. One must learn complete indifference to the conditions about one. When there is beauty and comfort, enjoy it; when discomfort, forget it. Indifference to bodily comfort is indeed the requirement of every soul who seeks high adventure, whether he be an explorer or a warrior.

So too is the detachment from the bondage of personal love a quality of both warrior and explorer since only can achievement be made when personal love is subordinate to the goal in question. Insofar as the love is an inspiration to greater achievement, it is good; but insofar as it acts as a drag upon initiative, it is bondage.

The goal of divinity is indeed a goal of high adventure, for a man ventures all he possesses of worldly happiness, pleasure and comfort to win the unknown and but dimly visioned prize. So has this world been conquered, by men of strong soul and clear vision, indomitable courage and purpose. So only shall the higher worlds be won by souls of high purpose and courage in the greatest of all human adventures and with the greatest of all rewards for achievement — winning Godhood, the supreme adventure.

When the man has chosen the Path, has subordinated all desires to this one great purpose, has freed himself mentally from the bonds of personal happiness and comfort, he is ready to attempt the perilous ascent. As an explorer prepares himself by study of the conditions he must face — by learning the language needful, by gaining perfect physical fitness — so the man who seeks the Path, the most dangerous of all adventures, must do likewise.

He must study the available information upon the Way, he must fit himself in mind and body for his task, for this great task of spiritual achievement requires the utmost expenditure of force in every direction and requires physical, mental and moral fitness in the highest degree. No man who seeks the North Pole can endanger his success by physical indulgence or moral slackness or mental inefficiency. The price of inefficiency and weakness is death. In the adventure of all adventures — the discovery of God — inefficiency leads to disaster, despair and madness.

With the recognition of the Way and the method and the training necessary comes also the need to understand that back of all evolution is fundamental unity and that unity is love.

One's duty is to achieve the high destiny of mind; but when achieved, it adorns not oneself but rather becomes another jewel in the crown of our Solar Lord for his use and service. Indeed, we reach our goal at last only by overpowering love for the principles of Goodness and Light, Love and Compassion which are behind all form.

As a man cognizes and seeks *That,* he comes to possess the universal tenderness and compassion which are the mark of spiritual age and maturity. This compassion is not necessarily tenderness to the form in which the spiritual man dwells, that form which often arrogates to itself its divine guest's prerogatives, but to the evolving spirit of man. Compassion fills the awakened man with a passion to free other bound souls and to awaken them to a vision of the goal.

Often man's greatest enemy to his spiritual growth is his personal self, and compassion cannot be shown to the prejudices and peculiarities of that unworthy instrument. Compassion in its truest sense inflicts discipline upon the personality that it may thus relinquish its paralyzing grip upon the soul.

As the Plan unfolds to the awakening spirit, the wonder and beauty of it amazes, and reverence for the patience of the Guiding Spirit and awe at the courage of Divine Man flame up. This love and reverence are expressed in many methods of service and in sincere desire to help man upward.

There are two great motives which lead man to the occult path, to the search for the hidden truth in the universe. One rises from a spiritual distaste for the world, a weariness of soul which makes him long for the eternal; the other from a great love for humanity and the desire for service. This latter may teach man to renounce the world and all personal desire for the sake of human betterment.

In order to succor the suffering world, he will offer all that he has and devote himself to the study of the Path of Wisdom and to achievement upon it that he may bring light to the world. This is the path of devotion and the one most easy for women. They, whose great motive power is devotion, service and sacrifice, find in this path the fulfillment of their natures. There are also those souls in masculine bodies who lean to the great Mother side of evolution, and they too follow this line.

It is, of all, the safest and surest path for it lessens the danger of arrogating spiritual power to personal ends, the line of danger, the line of destructive forces which endanger the soul's link to the body. When the devotion that women have felt for their children is kindled by the cry of suffering humanity and they feel their motherhood for all the sons of men and their responsibility for the race, they will advance rapidly, and through their efforts much will be done for mankind.

Salvation for the race lies in mankind. Only man's help to man can save himself and his brothers. Evil is caused by the evil in man's own heart. Man suffers not from the blows of nature without himself, but from the corrupt and evil civilization which he has built. Only he can remedy it and build a civilization which is an honor to himself.

In this, woman will help him. After her child-bearing period, she has energies and time to devote to the world that men often have not. She has practical experience in keeping harmony and in dispensing justice to a group of individuals. When her wisdom is applied to problems of state, much can be learned, much gained.

Because the cycle has turned to the point where many women are developing minds which seek interests beyond their own tiny circle, progress can be made with their assistance. The tremendous mother principle which is theirs by right of their sex can leaven the lump of suffering, ignorance and crime. It is a cosmic force which, turned to the use of humanity, can achieve miracles.

The first hindrance to progress which must be removed is that which blinds the human mind to the purpose of life. Material conditions cannot improve until the soul of man is awake, and with that awakening he sees his responsibility to other souls. The conditions of civilization which are most lamentable have arisen in the past through the unkindness of man to man. These conditions will be ever renewed until the souls of men awake.

However wisely and skillfully great minds may build civilizations, these civilizations cannot endure so long as corruption in men's hearts perverts the wisest of forms to serve their selfish purposes. "Seek ye first the kingdom of God, and all these things shall be added unto you." As man becomes spiritually awakened, he will save himself and his brothers from the suffering which ignorance, selfishness and indifference have shackled upon the world.

Therefore, awakening the soul in others becomes the paramount desire in the man, himself awakened, since only through this awakening of souls can peace and happiness come upon the Earth.

CHAPTER 4
The Battleground

The work of the chela on the probationary path, that path which he enters when he turns his face irrevocably to the goal, is guided by two forces: that of the Teacher or Guide who gives from time to time general instructions and warnings which bear upon the nature of the tests to come and that of the testing agents, or dugpas, who are given freedom by the ego to test the personality.

Until the time of probation, there are certain magnetic protections about personalities formed partly by the ego, partly by the great groups of spiritual men who throughout the ages have built reservoirs of power for the purpose and partly by the magic of the esoteric side of religions.

These shells or insulating walls — note the guardian angel summoned by baptism — protect the personality from assaults of the most destructive elementals of nature. The man is exposed inevitably to the changing currents of human moods — anger, lust, greed, cruelty, fear and hatred — but he is safeguarded from the malicious and destructive nature forces by humanity's guardians.

This protection, however, ceases to avail if certain conditions are brought about: first, use of drugs or alcohol in excess — a reason for the greatest care in use of drugs even in operations; second, association with those already obsessed by these entities, as in lunatic asylums and in dens of vice; third, the use of certain occult practices for awakening the kundalini prematurely. This burns out the guardian sheath.

In regard to the second condition, in time it will be recognized that lunatics vary in type. Those possessed of devils should not associate with those whose brains merely have weakened. Also their attendants should be changed frequently. Brutality and cruelty in asylums are largely due to the influence upon the attendants and doctors of the malicious entities surrounding the insane. All lunatics should be given much exercise in the open air and taught to work in the ground. This harmonizes them and brings them in touch with the counteracting nature forces of a constructive kind.

Unless exposed to one of these three dangers, under ordinary conditions man is protected. But when he seeks to become a chela, he is of necessity given some of the tests to prove him fit to become an assistant of the guardians of humanity. He must prove his power not only to resist attacks upon him but to control the power of these destructive forces.

Gradually, therefore, the shield is withdrawn and he finds in himself suddenly many qualities of which he had no cognizance, startled into activity by the instrumentality of the dugpas — evil elementals. This is a necessary step.

Yet, since fear of the dark forces is dangerous, often the warnings given chelas are of a general moral nature because stimulation from dugpas usually begins to manifest by moral delinquency. If a man truly fulfills his moral obligations as voiced in any of the great religions, he cannot fall into serious danger.

A man must know, finally, that all forces, both good and evil, lie within his own nature. These he must control and use. Uncontrolled force falls into vice, yet those forces which gravitate into vice and violence in the early stages of evolution are just those which make his evolution possible and which give him control, finally, over nature's more constructive forces. "The kingdom of heaven is taken by storm."

Our virtues are negative, our powers positive. These balanced make a man divine. But a chela should not adventure upon the path until his virtues are strong enough to sustain him, as otherwise the increase of power opens the door to the downward way of vice. The path of occultism is strewn with wrecks, verily, since too soon or too unprepared man has challenged the destructive forces which he must conquer ere he can tread the Path.

The teachings of the Buddha and of the Christ — gentleness, serenity, virtue, detachment — are the surest safeguards on the Path; and true devotion, unmixed with self, is the safest line of progress. The dugpas cannot trap a selfless man — compassionate, humble and devout. Let man beware of seeking to tread the Path too soon lest the forces there met awake within him sleeping devils before he has gained the strength of soul to conquer. Then, in truth, the destructive forces turn and rend, and disaster comes.

During this period of temptation all the forces of nature, within man and without him, rise to test his unselfishness. In the history of every great teacher we find this period described. However great may be the temptations of the world to the ordinary man, they are as nothing compared to temptations and dangers which beset the man who has challenged the hidden side of nature by seeking conquest on the Path of Initiation.

One should be slow, therefore, to judge too harshly the apparently disastrous failures of occult students who have dared greatly and not too wisely.* When exposed to the power of destructive forces, the chela becomes the battleground of Kurukshetra in which the forces of the personality, built through the ages of combat and selfishness on the involutionary path, struggle with forces of the spirit which seek to master them. It is that this mastery may be

*A reference to premature stimulation of the sleeping kundalini prior to preparation and purification of the various vehicles of consciousness. Partial purification of the emotional and mental natures of distortion and evil tendencies is seen as necessary for the safety and well-being of the chela. Also, the will is consciously directed to create safe boundaries for the potential charge of force kundalini provides. —CEP

complete, that the spirit may prove its power and marshal its forces as rapidly as possible that the destructive forces are brought to bear upon the personality to awaken in it all latent seeds of good and evil.

The full nature must be brought to maturity, cleansed, purified and set to service. The force of anger mastered becomes a titan harnessed. Science is gaining control over destructive elemental forces of nature — not only controlling destruction but controlling it by turning that power to useful purposes.

Similarly, forces within the nature of man — which when uncontrolled are dangerous and therefore in the unevolved man are left slumbering as long as possible — in the chela must be roused that he may conquer and control them and gain thereby his heritage of mastery over nature.

That wrath which in the uncontrolled man leads to violence, to murder, to cruelty is the source of power which wisely directed gives man control of destructive forces. That power for passion, which in its earlier stages manifests as sensuality, is the strong root buried in the mud which shall flower into divine compassion. That greed which makes a man gluttonous and selfish will in time develop the energy of intelligence and forethought which shall bring all nature into subjection.

These three great powers liberate the energy with which he will achieve divinity. In their crude form they are destructive, but like fire or electricity or water, when harnessed, they prove man's most dynamic agents for the service of humanity.

Not only do outward circumstances bring difficulties into life which only courage, coolness and endurance can surmount, friends fail and enemies become peculiarly bitter; but within man's own nature awaken demons of destruction which rise like ghastly spectres of an unholy past.

Man unites within himself both the destructive power of demons and the constructive power of angels. When these two are held subservient to his master will, pledged to the service of God and man, he has gained that conquest of self which makes him a Master, and the powers of nature are obedient to his will.

A man is Master not only by virtue of his control of elemental forces in nature, not by his feats of magic, not by his powers of vision and prevision, but by his conquest of the forces in his own nature. From the battleground within himself he knows evil and he knows good; he knows temptation and he knows conquest; and he stands steadfast, poised and masterful, directing these forces by his awakened will.

When he has learned to direct wisely these forces within himself, he can likewise direct them in nature. No man can master what he does not understand, and the great atonement of spiritual teachers comes from understanding the sinner's problem. Theirs the power to conquer the force which others still fail to do, and sharing the strength won in past conflict helps those still prostrate to arise and to assail victoriously the ancient foe.

The tests of the chela are mostly inner ones. Often when the battle is raging most furiously within, outwardly his life may be calm and untroubled. He must learn to lose himself in work, not necessarily world-shaking activities of which every ardent young soul dreams but often the daily drudgery which must be glorified by the spirit in which it is done.

Washing dishes becomes a holy thing when done in a spirit of prayer and sacrifice. When we serve man, we serve God. Jacob Boehme was a cobbler, yet the glory of his life illumined dark pages in medieval history. The test of the chela is his power to do well, happily, joyously that task before him — however humble and obscure.

Messengers are sent into the world in all ranks of life that the leaven of spiritual wisdom may reach all types of people. Many who could not find the presence of an exalted teacher are reached by a humble one. What a man is determines his worth, not what he does. The mark of the

Master is spiritual greatness of soul, not power of mind or success in politics, religion or science. Not by his powers — mental or occult — do we know him, but by his inner majesty of spirit. Magicians of various orders may achieve phenomena and do. Only a noble and masterful spirit can radiate spiritual power.

CHAPTER 5
The Chapels of Silence

We have seen that the preliminary training of the pupil is carried on upon the inner planes where he is taught the purpose of life, the vision of the goal and the methods, in a general way, to reach the goal. From the teaching which filters through from the inner planes to his waking consciousness, the pupil or aspirant learns to orient himself in life so that the goal of liberation dominates his actions.

In him is awakened, likewise, the spirit of compassion which must guide him safely through the perilous way of the Path. When the spirit of compassion and the desire for service to the world, or service to God, have been fully awakened, when the man has oriented himself to the goal and has adjusted himself mentally, morally and physically to the accomplishment of his purpose, he passes out of the preliminary classes of the inner planes and enters definitely into a third group of classes, those which teach specifically the training of the vehicles.

The first class is to awaken the man's spirit to recognition of the laws of evolution and the purpose of life. The second group began his training and taught him control of the vehicles. The third is open only to those who have proved themselves earnest and dedicated, who have passed the preliminary tests and pledged themselves to follow the light at any cost.

In the third group of classes experimental work is done in dealing with conditions on the inner planes. Usually two years elapse in preparatory classes before entering the third group. During this preparatory period many fall away. The rest devote themselves to study, to gaining self-control and to the practice of virtues.

At the end of that time, however, they are held to have sufficient knowledge to permit them to work with others already trained, so they are detailed to assist various groups engaged in active work. Among these groups are the invisible helpers who meet newcomers from the Earth and who act as guardians for special souls pledged to service in the world and needing, therefore, protection lest some accident cut short their usefulness.

There are groups too who try to keep clean and shining certain areas connected with the physical plane where light from the inner planes can radiate and where students may gain help and inspiration.

Groups of pupils are divided also according to their need for training. Maps are made of their characters, plotting their qualities and weaknesses so they may know themselves. The development of certain qualities is marked for immediate attention. Then karma is so adjusted to give them conditions in which these qualities can be developed most easily — as, for instance, courage or persistence or patience or self-control. Difficulties and problems arise in the outer life which will demand the development of the required quality. If the pupil meets these successfully, he will rapidly achieve the progress desired.

He should, therefore, look upon these difficult conditions as special opportunities vouchsafed to him whereby he can make more rapid progress. It is hard, often, when one is seeking to lead a more spiritual life to find daily problems suddenly intensified. But this intensification marks the attention of the ego, turned to pressing its personality forward. Difficulties then are opportunities, not penalties. If a man can surmount these difficulties and develop within himself powers which will permit him to meet with harmony the trials of daily life, he will rapidly clear away the obstacles in the path of his progress. At this point also begins the special training of disciples for specific types of work.

Upon the inner planes are found the Chapels of Silence, where echoes of the cosmic song can be heard. It is here that interplanetary exchange takes place, where the Lodges in charge of the planets of our solar system report progress and exchange greetings.

Used for various purposes, these Chapels have about them a magnetic sheath which isolates them from contact with vibrations of the three worlds — such as Devachan, or the heaven world, is isolated from pain and suffering of our planet, that wearied souls may rest.

The heaven world is a place of retreat, of joy and refreshment of spirit where those souls who labored hard in physical life may find refreshment before beginning once more their arduous labors in human incarnation. The heaven world is a guarded spot protected from all evil and all pain, established through the compassion of Great Beings in the earlier history of the planet when conditions on Earth were even more terrible than they are now and where only the prospect of future happiness and peace in heaven made it possible to endure the agonies and cruelties and anguish of Earth life.

The Chapels of Silence are used on special occasions at specific times as receiving stations for vibrations from other planets, and chelas are trained to receive these vibrations. At other times chelas are sent there for meditation. The stillness and isolation from other thoughtforms permit the bodies to be tranquilized, and the chela can gradually cleanse the vehicles of self-initiated activities until they become tranquil and limpid.

When this occurs, he can in a curious way see into his own vehicles and study their structure, texture and characteristics or qualities and so learn much about himself and his own problem. He begins to know himself and to see the plan of his evolution. It is similar to what the ego achieves at death.

Structure means the basic type of response to vibration in the vehicles. Texture indicates the fineness or coarseness of the matter drawn into them. Quality or character means the varying powers of mind and emotion built in by the virtues and vices.

In the Chapels of Silence one learns to see himself as he truly is. Every man has a fundamental response to life which is his keynote, the keystone of his arch, determined by his ray and sub-ray. First he discovers whether he is interested in the form and building the form or in the thought which lies behind and ensouls the form.

This is a very fundamental difference which continues up to the Godhead itself. In all nature, in all of evolution there are the two great forces at work — one shaping the form, one unfolding the spirit — and these two working together are the secret of all manifestation and of all progression.

Every man must be allied to one side or the other in his final analysis. All artists, all gardeners, all surgeons and many doctors, all builders respond to the building of form. All teachers, spiritual and clerical, most political leaders, writers, philosophers, scientists, soldiers respond to the spur of spirit or mind.

The structure may differ also in this way. One man may interpret all things in terms of color, another of sound, another of form; one may be geometric in his thoughtforms, another create more indefinite flashes of light; another may link rather with human feelings and characteristics and interpret vibrations in terms of man; another may interpret in terms of nature, akin to the spirit expressed in mountains, trees, fields. As was said, it is determined by the sub-ray or sub-plane to which a man has attuned himself.

In these Chapels of Silence the disciple slowly begins to see himself as if reflected in a mirror. He learns the keynote of each vehicle, first of the three lower belonging to the personality: body, emotions and mind.

Frequently each vehicle manifests a different one of the three gunas, or attributes: activity, rhythm and stability. Some have activity of the body; some, activity of the emotions; some, activity of the mind. Some have activity of all three. In other cases the dominant quality of the dominant vehicle shadows or reflects itself in the other two.

Intense mental activity of the lower mind usually manifests as restlessness in the physical body, uncontrolled activity in the mind — that is, not slow, sequential reasoning. Activity in the emotional body also shows itself in action, but rather in impulsive actions and in the need for excitement than in restless physical activity. This is often a failing of women.

Rhythmic vibration in the lower vehicles makes a pleasant vibration for all near that person, but it often means lack of power in the mind. It brings instability and indecision. If, however, intuition is aroused, this may be active and accurate.

In any case, the disciple is not desired to change the type of activity, but rather to develop its highest qualities, control and apply them. Slowness of mind serves concentration and continued effort. The mind does not tire easily, and makes the deep student. Swiftness of mind brings alertness and action in emergencies — the executive. Rhythm brings justice but often indecision. Stability in the vehicles often reflects itself as stubbornness and obstinacy, and the inability to learn quickly. But it means endurance, steadfastness and usually loyalty. In each case a balancing point must be sought where the best qualities of the type of vehicle are used and counterbalanced.

It must be clearly understood that the three gunas — action, stability and rhythm — are manifestations of three types of force which exist in the universe, no one of which can be said to be better than the other; they are merely different with distinct uses and qualities.

Rajas, or action, can be likened in the physical world to electricity; inertia or stability to the unmoving strength of mountains; and rhythm to the ceaseless movement of the sea. Often rhythm is interpreted as harmony; in actuality it is only the intermediate balancing force of the three.

Then too a man must learn to know the dominant force in himself — action, will and desire or intelligence. The main source of motive is kama manas, mind colored by desire — ambition and love being the two common forces, masculine and feminine, and almost equally selfish.

These manifest themselves in the three vehicles. Ambition in the physical manifests as ambition for physical power; in the astral or emotional, as ambition for domination over others — one pole of cruelty; in the mind, as ambition for conquest in the mental world.

Love manifests, first, in the physical body as sensual indulgence; second, in the astral as an intense sex nature, a constant demand for attention; third, in the mental as desire to feel one's sex power over men or women regardless of the pain inflicted. Here the dominant note is astral — sex desire. These are, of course, the low types of the forces.

These two great forces, love and ambition — replicas of buddhi and manas, negative and positive — manifest, modified however by the types of matter in which they work on each plane.

As the student learns to know himself, as he learns his tools, he learns also what qualities he needs to protect him from the shadow of his powers. And these he seeks to unfold. Being violent and destructive, activity needs poise and tenderness. Inertia or stability needs energy roused by the motive of devotion. Rhythm needs steadfastness, perseverance. Each ray and sub-ray has its compensating ray or quality which must be developed to establish balance.

It is the purpose of teachers to instruct each man to know himself — to know his type, his way or line of evolution and his strength and weakness. The purpose is not to change the type but to develop it to its highest point of efficiency.

To do this, the powers peculiar to his ray must be unfolded and at the same time the necessary safeguards to the dangers of that ray built in so that through his training a man may become efficient, balanced and dependable.

When the disciple has entered the preliminary classes and passed through the preliminary training outlined so that he has begun to gain some control over his vehicles, he is taken night after night to special, magnetized parts of the inner worlds where forces can be played upon him which will result in definite stimulation of certain of the vehicles.

After the disciple has learned somewhat about himself and has made the first steps in knowledge of the Self in the preliminary classes and in the Chapels of Silence, he is given into the charge of a chela who carries out a program laid down by one of the Masters, receiving the disciple each night and accompanying him on his pilgrimage to the centres allotted for that night.

In this way the pupil visits museums where replicas of ancient ceremonies are on view in order to stimulate in him memories of forces and truths gained in earlier lives. Usually a pupil approaches Theosophy because of a memory that has been aroused of some past life which marked occult progress for him. One of the surest ways of holding him to the Path is to permit that occult memory to be vivified and the atoms responsive to it stimulated. Flashes of the past then come in waking consciousness as feelings or thoughts, even as pictures.

It has the effect often, however, of causing the pupil to choose from the present teaching only that which is similar to the work and outlook of the past. This is dangerous, as in each age — owing to the magnetic polarity of the period and the change in the forces playing about the Earth's surface and through the races of men — new methods must be used. The forces must be handled differently. The polarity and construction of men's bodies differ in each age and race, and likewise the forces available for use differ. One must adapt oneself to the new age.

After the old memories are well aroused — sometimes of more than one life, lives in Egypt, India, Persia, wherever the Light was dominant and occult teaching available — the disciple is given the opportunity to try to awaken some of the powers and knowledge he had of old. Sometimes this is most successful and inner worlds begin to unfold to the waking consciousness in a way to give confidence to the man.

These early experiences, however, should not be given too much weight. They are but broken memories which are vivified in order to assure the waking consciousness of the reality of the inner worlds. True vision comes later — vision of work now on hand or to be attained in the future. Fragments of the past must not establish ancient habits of thought and feeling which would not be suitable to the present unfoldment.

The next step is establishment of certain qualities in the character which balance vices: for anger, tenderness; for sloth, passionate devotion; for selfishness, compassion.

When the pupil has gained knowledge of himself and his needs, he is shown the three paths of action, wisdom and will. Action, or karma, takes him finally into the class called the Masters, whether upon this planet or another, who are the direct agents of the Law upon each planet. Wisdom takes him into the Nirmanakaya class, working with the spirit of things, the forces which play upon all evolving life. The Nirmanakayas fill the reservoirs which supply spiritual forces to the world and upon which the Members of the White Lodge and Their chosen instruments may call for the benefit of man and of the planet. They control the magnetic currents about the Earth.

The third path, that of will, is one rarely chosen. It has to do with the work of the Kumaras, Who are the Guardians of the powers of the planet and the Arbiters of the destinies of nations and of continents. They become the ultimate judges of good and evil, holders of the keys of power whereby destruction is loosed upon the planet when the nice balance between good and evil, which is necessary to evolution, becomes endangered by the over-balance of evil.

At such times they loose upon the planet those forces which result in cataclysms and which destroy the evil centres on the Earth. They have in their hands the carrying out of the decrees of doom. They control the destructive forces in the universe and loose them when need arises.

CHAPTER 6
The Tests of the Probationary Path

A chela's advance is determined by the rapidity with which he can meet and conquer the forces of his nature and by the speed with which the destructive elemental forces of the planet may safely be loosed upon him.

Usually the first onslaught is the most destructive. If he passes and conquers this, he progresses rapidly. If, however, the defeat is not complete, he is tested again and again through the years until he feels he is beset by furies, as indeed he is.

The greatest test is usually doubt. If doubt can be cast upon the truth of evolution and upon the reality of the Path, the very strength of man's will is nullified. There is no power to fight.

The next greatest test is personal love. When a man turns his face to the solitary Path of Discipleship, he must leave behind in spirit the mortal ties which bind him to Earth. Not less dear are loved ones, but for their sake as for his own must he loose the bonds upon his soul which bind him to the ways of Earth — not that he must leave those he loves but that he must cease to lean upon them or to centre his life about them.

The focus of interest must change, and the one dominating purpose of life, the fulfillment to the uttermost of the Law, must order his thought. More tender will he be, more unselfish in his love since now he gives all and seeks nothing. It is the change of the inner point of view that matters — the orientation to God. No longer are his loved ones his. They are but servants and children of God whom it is his privilege to love and to serve, but to them he may not cling, nor for whom may he grieve if the plan requires that they pass to other work.

This is the spiritual meaning of the *vow of poverty.* A man may hold millions in his control and yet be poor in spirit in that his life and all he has are dedicated to serve the world and held in trust for God.

The third test is that of anger or hatred. The disciple must learn to receive injustice, slander, betrayal — without anger or hatred. It is not his concern what others may do to him for the Law will bring justice on all points. But what matters is whether onslaughts by destructive forces through human agents can stir destructive forces within him — not others' attitudes to him but his to all the world determines his progress.

Indeed insult, injury, treachery are necessary steps in the occult life to prove a chela's character and strength. Hence, all spiritual teachers, great and small, are beset by traitors, false friends, vindictive enemies — even such as Judas in the story of Jesus. Judas is not only a historical person but a symbol of a universal truth. In a sense a man's enemies are his best teachers since they offer the tests which alone can assure his spiritual unfoldment. Suffering is the price of progress.

The point of view of the occult student upon the probationary path must of necessity differ somewhat from that of the average person of the world. When he first places his foot upon that narrow Way which leads to Initiation, of his own free will he challenges fate and demands from the gods the priceless gift of discipline.

This discipline must make of him not only a kindly and a good man but a wise man, a powerful man and, above all, a man who has been tested in every way for human weaknesses and conquered.

This does not mean that when a man becomes an Initiate he will be free from human weaknesses. On the contrary, some may be intensified. It does mean he has shown powers of stability, forbearance, compassion and desire for service to the world which prove him probably strong enough to resist some of the major temptations later on the way.

Perhaps the hardest test that has to be passed successfully is this test of hatred and malice. A man must prove that neither injustice nor cruelty nor unkindness nor betrayal can rouse in him the desire for vengeance — must prove he is free from the terrible dangers of hatred. He may be hurt, he may be angry, he may feel injustice, but he must accept these without hatred.

It is necessary to change one's point of view, expecting not justice but tests. A man must meet disappointment and betrayal — actual or seeming. He may meet these things perhaps from those he loves most. It may be in fact, it may be only in seeming, but the test must be met and passed. In the end the Akashic Records show the truth, and he will be judged accurately to the last tiny act. We may all rely upon that law to bring us full justice.

Therefore, it matters not if we seem unjustly treated; it matters only whether we be just to others. When conditions are hard and when comrades fail, love betrays and friendship falters, let us look upon it as a testing necessary before we may feel our feet firmly planted upon that upward way which leads to Liberation. Until we have been tried to the uttermost, we cannot know our own strength, nor can those Wise Guardians of humanity depend upon us to help Them in Their great task.

Therefore, when we meet injustice, let us bear no resentment to those who so act, but laugh and recognize it as a clever test of the gods which we have demanded. It is sometimes hard to remember this when suffering the indignities of persecution, but it is nevertheless an inevitable part of the Path, and these tests may be more lightly and surely passed if one learns to avoid self-pity and to look upon hardships as opportunities, not penalties.

In the long distant future, when we look back from the heights of Adeptship upon the trials of the personality, we shall realize the greatest opportunities of progress were given us not by our friends but by those who seemed our enemies who, by their apparent injustice and cruelty, gave us the opportunity to pass the tests required by the upward Path of Initiation.

During the training and testing of the disciple on the probationary path, his progress is watched and recorded by a Master or by a high chela. The sum of efforts, of failures and of successes is recorded and, according to the balance of these, is increased force given. Those who have earned by dedication in past lives and by renewed efforts in this the power to hear the Master's voice are given from time to time in meditation counsel, admonitions or encouragement.

The disciple must be tested; such is the Law. But the Teachers watch with hope, almost prayerfully, his ascending steps. Every successful disciple who treads the Path to the Portal of Initiation marks a reward to the Teachers' age-long labors and lightens the load of Their responsibility.

No one could be more tender, more solicitous, more eager for the success of a pupil than these Elder Brothers Who have pledged Their lives to the service of man incarnation after incarnation. Yet in the crucial hour of test for which the pupil has been prepared with counsel and training, They must stand aside and let the test prove the disciple's own strength and intuition.

As in the world, the teacher may not help or counsel the pupil during an examination, nor may the Master guide the blinded steps of the disciple during the hours of test. The disciple must prove his own strength alone, his steadfastness, wisdom and intuition under the assaults of blindness, destructive anger, hatred, ambition and doubt.

When a pupil has definitely sought the probationary Path and turned his face to the goal of divinity, when he has proved his earnestness and dedication, he is allowed to draw upon the Master's forces for inspiration, strength and encouragement. As he reaches upward with love and aspiration, the Master pours out His strength to help the disciple.

But when the hour of test is come, the Master withdraws His aid that the inner strength of the disciple be proved. If the pupil reaches the Master then, it must be by his own unaided efforts that he break through the barriers of the destructive forces which have been permitted to come about him. This is the test or series of tests.

Can he break through the mists which surround and blind him and progress upward into eternal Light? If he can, then does he find the Light shining within himself — the true Light he seeks and which alone can illumine the Path as he progresses. Each time he breaks through the mists of illusion thrown about him, the Light within surges and increases its steady glow. Another facet of the divine jewel has been polished, to remain ever as a testimony of man's divine heritage.

As the chela passes the tests successfully, as he proves his capacity to stand alone, to follow the Vision, to find the Light within, he begins to be drawn closer to the Master and to share in His work.

More power is available for the chela's use since it has been proved he can be trusted to react well to its stimulation. He begins to enter his period of service in which he distributes the Master's force or, more accurately, a small portion of the force of the White Lodge, either in active service in the outer world or in intimate contact with those about him.

The use of this force expands and develops his vehicles and their powers. His brain increases in power, his devotion in intensity and purity, his actions in accuracy, skill and force. Moreover, he becomes more radiant — a luminous, serene and joyous figure in the dark atmosphere of worldly life.

At the same time, he begins definite training on the inner planes where he is taught the use and control of forces there. Little by little he gains knowledge of the control of various elements, of elementals connected with them and of devas in charge of the elementals.

In all these things he is taught how to command the services of deva and of elemental in the name and by the authority of the White Lodge, as an agent of Its Power. He must not by purchase, by bribe, gift or tribute gain the services of these forces, as many lesser ones do, to attain a modicum of magical power. He is taught the line of evolution of these elementals, the motive power of their action and the type of force which they obey. This differs for different elementals and devas. To accomplish this control, three things are needed.

> 1st: Serene courage which has no element of doubt or fear as to the power to control.

> 2nd: Absolute dedication in the use of the forces — using them only for the work, not for oneself or even for the pleasure of using them.

> 3rd: Serenity. Irritation and anger endanger the use of these forces. It disturbs the elementals and may cause them to turn and attack the one who commands them. It is similar to handling a swarm of bees.

Courage, serenity and dedication are essential. Many fail because in handling elementals they lose control of themselves and are therefore attacked by the forces they use — much as an electrical engineer might endanger himself if in a fit of irritation he jammed the machinery controlling the currents of high voltage.

When the chela has proved himself fit for advancement by carrying the Master's force successfully, by resisting attacks and surmounting the tests, he passes to the point of becoming an accepted disciple.

This means he will have access to the reservoirs of the Master's powers at any time to use for helping the work. He definitely will then begin to find the force he needs for service. While on probation, he has found at times a downpour of force to meet some special need. Now he can summon it at will.

When the pupil has passed the tests of the probationary Path and has been accepted by the Master Who will train and guide him, the Portal of Initiation opens before him. Beyond this Portal lie the shining peaks of achievement which shall lead him ultimately to God and to his heritage as a Son of God.

CHAPTER 7
Departments of the Hierarchy

The work of an accepted disciple differs from that of the probationer. He already has power to control circumstances so as to orient his life to occult laws. He has taken his character in hand and to some extent trained and educated and coordinated it, and he has shown some capacity for service in the world.

He is considered fit, therefore, for special training which shall prepare him safely to handle certain occult forces on the inner planes and to transmit those forces, in part at least, through his lower vehicles to the world of man.

There are two great ways of service among Adepts. One demands work principally on the physical plane — actual work among men, either in giving spiritual light to their minds directly as a teacher, or by organizing channels such as churches or schools, or by actually sharing in the reform work politically and socially which is going on in the world.

The other way consists of work, entirely or almost so, upon the inner planes: building reservoirs, stimulation of occult centres, manipulating magnetic currents and other planetary forces; directing forces in nature which affect climatic conditions and change the form of continents.

To some extent both kinds of service are required of the chela. The proportion of inner and outer plane work depends upon what his future is to be when he reaches the Adept level. If he is going to become a Master — that is, one who works directly with members of the human race —

a large part of his work as a disciple will be with men upon the physical plane.

The work of the Adept who becomes a Master is quite different from that of one who does not. A Master has a direct relationship with men; in fact, he is called "Master" because he takes pupils. He may hold official positions in the Hierarchy with regard to man — such as Manu, Bodhisattva and Mahachohan — or become one of the Officials of the Seven Rays; or he may share in the occult social structure, serving in one of the departments for the supervision and guidance of the race. These work primarily with men, with the consciousness of humans and their social and political forms and with the forces playing through humanity.

Besides the work with humanity, the work of each Manu, of course, includes establishing a continent suitable — in climate, flora, fauna and food, as well as magnetic conditions — for the development of the peculiar traits and characteristics which His people must manifest.

This work is only undertaken after He has reached a very high level and consists in laying down plans and specifications which must be followed by nature workers and the builders of organic and inorganic forms, rather than the manipulation of the forces themselves.

When the time arrives for his work, He summons from occult laboratories hundreds of specialists who have been experimenting along the lines of continent building for thousands of years and into their hands places much of the responsibility for carrying out the plans. His major work consists in hammering masses of men into shape.

By playing one group against another socially and politically, the right balance of nations under His control is kept — by contest and struggle, as well as by peace and prosperity and various arts which follow therefrom. He must develop certain qualities in His people according to the Plan laid down for Him by the Ruler of the Planet and according to the Plan laid down for the Ruler of the Planet by the Archetypal Logos, Who supervises planets of a certain type and bent of evolution in a given group of solar systems.

Although our Logos is in direct charge of His own Solar System, He invokes the aid of other high Logoi Who have specialized in certain types of evolution in the past and Who are, as it were, Advisory Experts to various Logoi in relation to difficult parts of the solar evolution. All this has to do with the manifested side of evolution on the physical plane.

A Manu is undoubtedly a great occultist, but one primarily Who knows where to enlist the services He needs and to requisition the knowledge necessary for building His kingdom. Whereas kings rule over one kingdom for a lifetime — made up often of various states, all subordinate to their authority — the Manu's kingdom covers the birth and growth of a great Root Race and includes many civilizations, nations and empires within it. Nevertheless, there is a close similarity between the duty and functions of the ruler of an empire and those of a Manu.

Those Initiates who work to bring about the form side of evolution usually become Masters, often heads of the department under the Manus and ready to take pupils either to prepare them for given work under the Manu or for the particular work of the department in which the Masters Themselves are active.

Included under the department of the Manu and race building are the departments of the Bodhisattva and the Mahachohan, with all their various ramifications. All this is primarily work in the world of man and with the various forces — elemental and otherwise — working through man and the kingdoms associated with man.

But another great line of evolution works primarily with the inner forces. Closely associated with the work of the devas, the Adept who follows it nearly approximates some of their work. It deals not only with building great reservoirs for storing power — magnetic, spiritual and elemental — but it includes the actual development of the forces of nature on the inner and outer planes, latent in matter.

When they reach the Adept level, chelas destined for this kind of inner plane work begin at once their training in handling occult forces. These forces are quite different from the forces used by humanity and dedicated to its service. They are related rather to the evolution of the planet itself and to opening occult centres in the Planetary Body.

This department deals with many strange and mysterious things — forces not only emanating from the great Power House in the centre of Earth but from various sheaths which make up the physical, etheric, emotional and mental bodies of the planet.

In such sheaths certain forces are latent which must gradually be evolved and unfolded so planetary growth may be harmonious and balanced. Those who work with these forces more nearly approximate in the Planetary Body the cells in the body and brain which control the subconscious in physical man.

Chelas on this line must learn to summon from the solar system and the whole Cosmic System special forces for use as need arises, much as the etheric body learns unconsciously to draw prana, or vitality, for the body's use — only in the large planetary plan the cells and centres represented in man by the subconscious are represented by conscious Entities Who direct this work.

Also the chelas experiment in learning to contact new inter-solar forces and make themselves foci whereby these forces can be distributed to the planet. Many strange things in this connection are still unknown to most of us. We touch but the fringe of that other consciousness, the subconscious, even in our own body and much less so in the Planetary Body.

Entities are brought from time to time from other regions and solar systems to instruct the planet and to help invoke unusual, hitherto unattainable forces. Then, slowly and with great caution, this second department of Adepts and Their assistants learns to develop in themselves conditions and vibrations which will permit them to transmit these forces for the planet.

Occasionally strange invasions and incursions from errant groups of destructive agents either arrive here by chance or are brought here to give planetary workers certain tests and trials. Great, then, are the calls for rapid action on the part of the Guardian Group in the Hierarchy.

Many evolutions in the planet have little or no relation to man. Perhaps humanity might be said to correspond to one group of cells in the Planetary Body, with one major function — perhaps the cerebro-spinal in certain aspects.

But we either do not recognize or cannot understand the existence of many others. After all, evolution of man is only incidental to evolution of the planet. Man profits by sharing in that evolution, but it is not primarily for his benefit that it exists. Elemental essence profits by being used by man for his own purposes of evolution, but it does not exist primarily for him; it is but one of the materials included in a vaster plan available for his temporary use.

So man's life and growth upon this planet contribute necessary elements to planetary growth, and through sharing in this growth and contributing these necessary elements to the intricate planetary life, he is permitted thereby to profit — through experience and through evolution — for himself.

It is to his advantage to shorten his stay in this particular stage as much as possible. He contributes to the well-being of planetary evolution most by hastening through it as rapidly as possible and by not delaying his growth or seeking to turn the forces too much to his own uses — for his evolution hastens all evolution.

Very much like a cell in the body, it is his duty to help carry on the planetary life, to fulfill his functions here and to make his contribution to the magnetic forces of the

Planetary Body. His happiness and well-being are dependent upon fulfilling this required service. All other pleasure or happiness is incidental and destroyed if it clashes in any way with the requirement of service.

A man who attempts to seize personal happiness or personal power at variance with this law of service to the planet becomes like a cancerous group of cells in the body at war with the needs of the whole body. If they become powerful enough to endanger the life of the whole, he or his group are cut out and destroyed if they cannot be reoriented to their duty.

It is this which happens in the periodical Days of Judgment, an example of which we have in the destruction of Atlantis and in the aeonic damnation of which the Christ warned in the Bible.

The need to fulfill a required service to the planet is the basis of teaching dharma. It is inevitable at this stage that men should seek personal happiness, but it is obtainable only as the result of fulfilling dharma — duty, service to the plan. All religions teach duty to God as the first requisite. The great teachers sought to put in simple form this law of the required service to the Planetary Logos, to teach man not to seek happiness in personal satisfaction.

Happiness comes only in carrying out the plan, and those are happiest who base their happiness upon the plan and not upon other humans. If humanity could once grasp the relation between happiness and this fulfillment of service, many grief-stricken hearts whose lives seem broken and useless would be at peace.

By living, just by living nobly, they serve the Law. Suicide in most cases is a sin against this fundamental law of obedience to and service to the Planetary Spirit. It is a soldier who falters in the great campaign.

CHAPTER 8
Occult Forces

The accepted chela becomes an outpost of the consciousness of his Master. In other words he begins to be called upon to distribute on the physical plane some of the forces the Master has at His command. This requires sensitizing the body in order to temper it, to make it responsive. The nerves must be tensed, like keying up a violin.

There are several methods of doing this. One is to live in a highly magnetized spot or in close contact with the Master. Another is intensity of joy and pain, either physical, emotional or mental or all three. However, as occult steps always require paying certain karma — debts — usually a clever adjustment is made so debts are paid and the suffering involved at once develops the necessary character qualities and sensitizes the nervous system.

As rapidly as possible the Master starts pouring force through his chela. As rapidly as possible also the chela learns on the inner planes to manipulate the forces necessary for this inner plane work. Little by little he is exposed to the impact of elemental currents from which the average man is protected until the chela proves himself able to meet these forces without wavering in any vehicle.

This is not as easy as it sounds. There are not only the primary elemental forces connected directly with man and playing through him for his development and evolution. These in themselves are powerful enough — as can be seen where uneducated groups are subjected to emotional impacts and mob psychology results; but man occasionally contacts greater currents by chance — not particularly related to man but belonging to other evolutions or to the life proper of the Planetary Spirit.

The force is stupendous, literally an inner world cyclone or high voltage power current. Many chelas, especially those who are to do outer plane work and become ultimately the guides and teachers of humanity, are required to understand only the human forces and those distributed on the planet for the use and help of man and his related kingdoms. Sometimes these chelas are said to belong to the branch who takes Initiation under the Planetary Group.

But playing through the planet are other forces which belong to the solar system and even the inter-solar scheme. These are present for development of the planet itself and those consciousnesses on the planet who are linked to the Inter-solar Group.

These forces, directed to the planet from vast distances and from centres entirely outside of our present solar system, are part of the inter-cosmic forces playing on our solar system as a whole for the evolution of our Logos and His chief associates.

Groups of His associates are established in the various planets partly to help His work, partly to carry on Their studies and Their own development through experience in administering these forces for the system and for the planet. These are the Kumaras of planets and Their associates Who form the Inner Council of Power.

Among those who achieve Initiation, a few seek to qualify ultimately for this special group and take the training. At each Initiation these are required not only to pass the tests in the ordinary planetary forces but also in the solar and inter-solar forces. A peculiar quality of will is required for this and manipulation in special ways of the elemental forces of earth, air, water and fire, so as to learn to change the inner vehicles in such a way that they can endure the play of the greater forces without being rent asunder; and also to form a protecting shell about the physical body, so that the residue of force in the inner vehicles after experimentation will not cause too severe a repercussion upon the physical when the sleeper awakes.

The chelas on this line work primarily with the forces of one of the four elements: earth, air, water and fire. They become experts, as it were, in one department. Earth magic is really planetary magic and more or less available to all Initiates. But water magic is very potent — one of the two primary creative elements, the other being fire.

Air is an offshoot of fire, as earth is of water. Air offers control of the forces of the planets of the solar system. Water enters into the ocean of space and gives access to inter-solar forces. Fire represents kundalini — creative power loosed in atomic motion — and gives access to almost all occult forces in the inter-solar scheme. The interplay of these two, fire and water, brings about all manifestation.

Also in the deva kingdom are divisions between those handling planetary and those manipulating inter-solar forces, one of which leads to the position of Chief Administrator of the Solar Forces and Director of the Inter-cosmic Currents. The devas have great responsibility as to the amount of force they summon from the solar system for the use of the planet — wisely to judge of this and wisely to distribute it so that harmonious relations of different parts of the planet and the evolving kingdoms on the planet will persist.

Much of their energy latterly has been given to counterbalancing as skillfully as possible the destructive forces that man has been loosing during the past five thousand years while he was passing through his period of unconscious darkness. Previous to this he cooperated with the devas either consciously or in obedience to religious laws laid down by wise teachers.

When Kali-Yuga began, however, this general cooperation ceased. All over the planet the positive and dynamic occult centres were sealed to prevent the outpouring of force which would increase man's destructiveness but which, when closed, greatly diminished his power. One reason for the great increase in disease during that period was the diminished vitality in man from closing these active centres in the world.

Thus, the work of keeping the world well balanced and tolerably clean devolved upon the devas alone, with a few rare exceptions among souls of transparent vision able to know the law and to cooperate. Religions became rationalistic or devout instead of being instructed, scientific and magical.

Only the negative reservoirs tapped by devotion, love, aspiration and self-abnegation were left available to man since those could not easily be misused to his own destruction during his period of ignorance and darkness.

CHAPTER 9
The Work of the Different Masters

As the accepted disciple begins to handle forces on the inner planes, the play of forces through the vehicles does two things. Because it unfolds the latent powers in him much more rapidly than in the average man — as the steady playing of warmth in a hothouse intensifies the growth of a plant — there are two results.

First, the play of force increases the vigor with which both virtues and vices manifest and intensifies the man's struggle with himself; secondly, this speeding up of the unfoldment of latent powers also automatically hastens the rate at which a man lives, so that he passes in a few years through the experience of a lifetime and in those few years lives through the karma of a lifetime. In this way he increases greatly the precipitation of karma, both good and bad.

The accepted disciple has definitely set out to achieve his goal — the unfoldment of divine powers within himself to the point required by evolution on this planet — as rapidly as possible and far more rapidly than the average man. He has pledged himself to endure the penalties exacted by that speed in achievement which are very great physically, morally and mentally; and he has pledged himself to use the powers as they unfold for the service of the world.

Calmness is the great requisite under the tension of expanding vehicles. Tests are given in different order, but some of them include tests in patience, pride, anger, conceit, fanaticism, detachment. There must be calmness of mind, of body, of emotion; there must be regularity of life, a definite pressure maintained upon the vehicles to control them and develop their powers harmoniously.

Excitement, restlessness, desire for results, passion, price, depression — all are stumbling blocks which must be overcome. There must be a calm, dispassionate purpose to build gradually the qualities and vehicles required day by day, month by month. The desire to work at once before training is accomplished, to *see* results, often defeats the purpose.

Training is the first step. Can an engineer be trusted to build until he has finished his training? This applies, however, only after one is on probation and under training. Earlier, acts of service prove a man's fitness for probation.

The first Initiation marks the point where the Master considers the pupil able to successfully receive the forces up to a certain voltage and has proved his capacity to turn this increased force to service; in other words he has reached the point where he can be permitted to enter as an independent member into that Brotherhood which distributes the forces governing the growth of the planet and has proved sufficiently trustworthy to have access to the reservoirs available for that Body.

When he has passed the fifth Initiation, he enters that Group which has to do with administering the forces of the planet and establishing reservoirs for the distribution of the Brotherhood. This Group has the responsibility of gathering into the planet from the solar system the forces It considers necessary for use in a given period and the allocation of those forces to the various departments, much as a government allots its budgets.

The work of the accepted disciple is to prepare as rapidly as possible to take his place in the Brotherhood. This is done by the triple action of controlling vehicles so they can handle the forces on the outer planes, of learning to handle the forces on the inner planes and of controlling his bodies under the repeated impacts of karma coincident with his growth.

In fact, development of the disciple depends upon the growth in him of strength, steadfastness and unselfishness — strength coming from the increased power in handling forces, steadfastness in the unshaken front with which he meets problems within himself and in his life precipitated by karma and unselfishness in the increasing capacity to turn all his powers to the service of the world.

His intelligence and discrimination must, at the same time, be constantly developing so he will learn wisely to use the force at his disposal. Just as a rich man must learn to administer his money wisely, so the occult student must learn wisely to allocate his time, his strength and his service. The world is not served by indiscriminately giving money to all who ask it. The administrator of public or private funds soon learns that to answer all appeals for money often does more harm than good.

In the same way, the work of the world is not profited by sympathy which permits one to become as it were a moral post upon which others lean. Every mother knows that if she loves her children wisely she will not grant all their requests and that the fibre of manhood is not built by overindulgence or by too much sympathy — encouragement, yes, and strengthening their wills, but not endless listening to the babble of self-pity and certainly not an attempt to prevent their meeting the consequences of their mistakes.

There has been a misunderstanding in the world as to the meaning of a spiritual teacher. To some the Christ was a Comforter. But to others He was a Flail of Righteousness, a retribution for their evil deeds. To some He gave pity and aid, but to others He gave tasks beyond their power to achieve, as in the case of a young man having great riches.

Men perhaps at times need comforting, but most of all they need assurance as to the goal and leadership in courage, in independence and in sacrifice of worldly considerations to attempt that goal. The Great Teachers come not so much to comfort us for our sorrows as to mark out the route of conquest whereby we may enter new worlds. It takes supreme courage and supreme strength to storm the gates of the Kingdom of God.

All who achieve Initiation, however, are not on their way to the attainment of Christhood or Buddahood. This is one office among many and requires peculiar qualifications which only the exceptional man, even among the Brotherhood, can achieve.

When a Christ enters upon His Great Office, His compassion must be so deep and His understanding of others so vast that His heart can be linked by invisible lines of light to every human heart on the planet, a towering figure of love, compassion and power. His consciousness reaches such lofty regions that He can transmit to this planet the Consciousness and the Power of the Second Person of the Trinity.

But in the work of the Hierarchy there are many departments, each requiring different qualifications and each carrying on a different branch of the plan. Not only have the Seven Great Officials of the Rays Their major departments and Their group of associated administrators for the distribution of the force of each ray, but within the scope of each department many sub-departments and many offices require specialization.

There are many Masters, but only one Christ, and the qualifications for His Office are not the qualifications for all offices. One may find a parallel in the work of a great nation, for after all the administration of a kingdom is based considerably upon the method of administering the planet, another evidence of the old saying, "As above, so below."

The king is the ruler of his people and the head of the government. The priest should meet the problems of man's emotional nature, giving him comfort and succor in his hour of tribulation. But other departments must be dedicated to the service of the state, contributing directly to man's ultimate welfare and to the welfare of the kingdom but rarely contacting the individual man at all.

Such a department is formed by great scientists who conduct researches which may ultimately benefit millions but who could not possibly do their work except in isolation and free from interruptions. They may have very little personal sympathy with or understanding of the problems of an individual man, although devoting their lives to the welfare of humanity.

The Masters are not all Christs or Christs-to-be. They fill posts in the complex government of the planet, posts won for Them by two great qualifications, equally necessary: the development of superior ability along special lines which made Them fitted to carry on Their special work, be it research or art or administration, and the willingness to sustain that work for the welfare of the world.

Sometimes one considers a Master merely a supremely good man. One forgets that to be a Master one must have mastered some function of human consciousness, and before one may be assigned to a post of responsibility in any world, one must have earned the right to the appointment by proven capacity. Virtue unaccompanied by knowledge and ability is of small service to humanity.

No man may attempt a degree of Master of Arts in any human university by good character alone — it must be accompanied by intellectual achievement; nor, on the other hand, can he attempt that degree if virtue is not the accompaniment of intellect. The same law holds good in all worlds, and the Christ Himself has achieved His lofty position not only by the practice of compassion but also by deep and prolonged study into the mystery of the human consciousness, so that He is an Adept in understanding the human heart, its motives, its trickeries, its treacheries, its sublime achievements and its pitiful failures.

It is well to remember that during His appearance in Palestine, His denunciation of the oppressors rose side by side with His compassion for the oppressed; there was not only His pity for the sinner but His righteous wrath against the hypocrites, called by Him in unmistakable language, "A generation of vipers."

Those Adepts Who are termed Masters, Those Who deal largely with masses of humanity and Who are responsible for their evolution along executive or religious lines, are the only ones Who take pupils in the general sense of the word.

The other Adepts, Who might be called specialists, usually have about Them each a small group of Their own line and type, fitted to share in Their peculiar work and ultimately to become Their successors when They leave the planet. These Adepts one does not contact until one has achieved a high degree of proficiency in one of the special lines of research, such as the manipulation of magical forces, profound knowledge of science or of music.

If one met such Adepts, it is doubtful They would be recognized as Masters for the dominant note would be science or abstract thought rather than compassion or power. Many of the chelas of these Adepts are distinguished less by the pure compassion of the Christ and the overflowing love associated with it than by dispassionate dedication of their services to the increase of knowledge for humanity.

CHAPTER 10
The Tests of the Accepted Disciple

It is to be remembered that the first Initiation marks progress only to the point where the major part of a man's efforts in life will be dedicated to the service of mankind and where also he will have achieved a certain capacity to guarantee that force put at his service will be used profitably.

In work for humanity it is the disposition of all forces at the command of the pupil which counts. Whether it be money, whether it be health, whether it be strength, whether it be sympathy, whether it be spiritual resources that he has, all must be disposed of to serve the greatest good of the greatest number, and to a very considerable degree his work for any individual must be limited by the value of the services that individual can render to the work of the Lodge.

It is often hard to realize the need for cool and dispassionate thought in the conservation of energy and in the wise disposal of one's time and resources. Initiates are primarily trustees, often with a given piece of work to do to which the major part of their energies must be directed and with only a small margin remaining for the casual requirements of friendship, associations and the general public.

Throughout the training of the chela he is tested for discretion, conservation, efficiency and economy, as well as dedication. His faults are judged more by how they interfere with his capacity for service than as factors in themselves. Almost all men have the weaknesses of their virtues, but these weaknesses are not judged by the conventional standards of the world.

Spite is far more seriously considered from the occult standpoint than the breach of conventional moral law, and the mind which rejoices in gossip less hopeful than one prone to anger. In the end a man must meet all the weaknesses of his character and must achieve control in every vehicle and on every plane of nature, but the order in which those faults are corrected is not determined by the conventional emphasis of the world, and sins which come from lack of control range far lower and do far less harm than those aligned to malice.

These latter sins are easily forgiven in the conventional world where gossip and slander are often reckoned as wit and where bigotry and intolerance pass for morality, but it is otherwise in the inner worlds. The measure of man's morality is determined by the nature of his faults, whether they arise from a mean and cruel streak in his character or are merely by-products of some great virtue not yet wholly governed.

The sweep of a wide and generous nature may often include failings which are unimportant hangovers from the past and yet which may be harshly judged by the creeds of narrow natures. In occult work bigness is necessary before all things — generosity of heart and mind and spirit.

The measure of a man's service is determined not by his faults but by what he accomplishes in spite of them, and narrow virtues often possessed by limited or still undeveloped natures may be swept aside and broken when the surge of a man's egoic power begins to pour through the channels of his mortal life.

Many a tranquil stream running quietly between well defined banks becomes a rushing torrent which ruthlessly sweeps away anything which opposes it on its way to its objective when the mountain snows add their volume of water to its own. So, many a controlled and balanced life surfaces in unexpected places under the down-pouring of new occult forces from the reservoirs of the Masters.

During the period when man is progressing from the point where he sets his foot upon the probationary Path until the time he has achieved the occult rank of Arhat, his work is intensively the work of preparation. He is like a man who has entered the university and who must graduate before he is really fitted to commence his greatest work in the world.

Such work as he does outside his curriculum must be a subsidiary outlet for his surplus energy and a means of preventing his becoming too self-centred. But his major effort must be directed to self-preparation that he may more rapidly become available for trained service.

In the same way, the work of the chela is primarily one of preparation. For the sake of the work he has to do, he must achieve as rapidly as possible. Sometimes, therefore, those who are making a great effort on the occult path may seem to be doing very little in the world. Judged from the standpoint of worldly achievement, they may have little to show.

None the less, those who can see into their inner consciousness know they are being subjected to tests of ever-increasing difficulty, that the vehicles are being strained to the utmost and that in some cases they are, as it were, upon the rack, tortured to the limit of their capacity to develop the sensitivity of mind and body needful for the work and at the same time to share, even though vicariously, the sorrows of human evolution in order to understand the human heart and thereby learn how to direct, guide and comfort humanity.

Increasing pressure from inner-plane forces strains the nerves intolerably, yet steadfastness and endurance must be learned. Every desire of personal life, little by little, must be burnt away, as dross is cleansed from gold. In most cases this is done by pain as the most rapid means to free the pure gold of the spirit from the dross of human weakness and desire. Renunciation after renunciation must be faced.

Often, none of this is apparent to the outer world, but within the consciousness of the chela the great fight is on, and the battleground, Kurukshetra, is his abiding place until every weakness has fallen before the increasing power of his will and his sacrifice.

Not only this. Not only must he conquer his own short-comings and control the elemental forces which play through his nature and are the heritage of evolution, but he must learn to find the Light within his own soul. Those warring forces built strength in the personality so spirit might have a powerful instrument when at last it conquered the unruly will of its lower nature.

He must cease to lean upon the Master or upon God; he must become God and feel the rise of divine power, of divine compassion and divine knowledge within his own heart. He must learn to stand uncomforted by any human love; he must learn to expect nothing from friendship and to give all. He must learn to accept injustice from the world without resentment, without surprise.

It is the law of the spiritual life that the man who wrests the treasures of occult knowledge and of occult power long guarded by the elemental for the service of man must pay the price. He must meet the anger of those elementals denuded of their sacred treasure, and he must meet the wrath of men glamoured by these elementals to wreak their vengeance.

Hints of this strange law have come down to us through the ages in various mythologies: in the story of Sigurd and the Treasure of the Dragon, in the Tale of Prometheus.

These tests do not all come during the period of disciple-ship, but they are foreshadowed in tests which the accepted disciple must meet, to be repeated in ever higher spirals as man progresses up the winding path to his goal.

It is because of the terrific severity of these inner tests given to those pressing forward to Initiation and beyond that the plea goes forth to all who glimpse something of the occult law:

Pour not the dross of criticism
Into the melting pot of discipleship.

All who tread the occult path are being tried beyond their strength, and they have need of the compassion and understanding of all students.

It is because the occult path brings much suffering; it is because the heart must be broken ere the personality relinquishes its will to the guidance of the ego; it is because those who have trod the Path even in small measure can scarcely endure the thought that others must suffer as they have suffered; it is because the Masters have anguished and bled and suffered; it is because They know the intolerable pain of evolution, that Their compassion is ever about the chela.

And when the darkness is greatest, when he seems to be utterly deserted alike by friend and Master, when he seems in a wilderness sombre and unillumined, utterly alone and hopeless even of God, then is the compassion of the Master most surely about him. For the Master understands in full the darkness and despair that accompany some of the steps on the upward Path.

If those who have trod the Path only in part — and who know something of the pain which is to come — have such compassion for those who must follow in their footsteps that they dread to have others face that which they themselves have undergone, in how much greater measure must the compassion of the Masters be stirred.

It is said that the Lord Buddha, when He finally achieved and looked back upon the dark and stormy path which he had trod, had almost "deemed it all too hard for mortal feet" until the Spirit of the Earth seemed to cry out, "Surely I am lost, I and my creatures; O Supreme! let Thy Law be uttered!"

The gateway of birth is fraught with agony, yet the physician must not stop the pangs but must impart courage to endure and to achieve; so only can the race persist. The gateway to the Kingdom of Heaven likewise is fraught with anguish, yet the Great Physicians cannot withhold the pain; They can only give courage to enter and to achieve. So only can the race achieve its heritage; so only can man pass from the bondage of the flesh to the liberation of the spirit.

Therefore, despite Their compassion — perhaps it is because of Their compassion — the race more speedily may pass along the appointed way, sooner to escape the suffering which the bondage of flesh exacts. Those who guide humanity stand by and let the tests be given.

Despite the anguished cry of the tortured heart, They permit the disciple to suffer; They leave him in darkness, alone and sometimes afraid, to find the Light; They give him more than his strength can meet, for so is new strength gained; They give him more than his heart can bear, for through the portals of the broken heart, the power of the spirit flows.

All this, and more, They do; for They would hasten and not delay the birth pangs of the spirit. Great Physicians of the soul, They seek to solace the world by urging men onward through the Gateway of the Kingdom for They know, as none but the Wise Ones of the Earth can know, that the only hope of lessening the anguish of humanity is through the Path which leads to life eternal.

PART IV
Preparation for Initiation

CHAPTER 11
Relation to the Master

The time comes when such progress has been made that a candidate must start to prepare himself definitely for Initiation. During all the period of accepted discipleship, the chela has been in close touch with some one of the Masters. This Master has undertaken to prepare him for Initiation. Before he was accepted as a disciple, he had fulfilled the preliminary requirements of the Master Who embraced him.

Every Master or teacher emphasizes the requirements a little differently. To some, certain qualities are paramount, and unless the candidate has them already to a marked degree, They will not even undertake his training. It is also probable that certain virtues are more important to one ray than to another. It may be this which determines the requirements of the various Masters.

When a Master undertakes to train a candidate, He takes a very great burden upon Himself. All those who apply for such training should bear this strongly in mind. The Master is a man in a human body with many of the limitations of a human body.

When He takes a new body, which He has to do repeatedly, He takes a body which is a child of the race with all the limitations and weaknesses which national consciousness, heredity and environment produce. He must take this very ordinary human body, train it and discipline it through many, many years until it is in some measure capable not only of carrying through the high voltage forces which He needs in His work but of reproducing, when necessary, upon a sensitized brain those plans for the future which are in the archetypal world, enough of which He must bring down to guide Him in practical work on the physical plane. These are more or less like an architect's drawings, a guide for the constructive work He is to do, and His ability to do that work well depends: first, upon the cognition of the plan; second, upon training His vehicles for use so He may influence directly or indirectly the humans and the nations with whom He is to work.

It is very doubtful whether any Master can do much with a new body until He has trained it for forty or fifty years. This, of course, is from the occult standpoint. If He is one of those upon the active rays who constantly reincarnates in the arena of active life, He may tune and train the vehicles only to the point where He can accomplish the particular job He has in hand.

In other words He may not make the effort necessary really to discipline and perfect the instrument so that it may be a suitable vehicle for His higher powers. He may not undertake to eliminate all of the human faults which are woven into the fabric in which He has clothed Himself and which belong to the race and to heredity; He may only discipline it sufficiently to meet the immediate need and then promptly drop it again as soon as the particular work in hand is over.

This is perhaps a hard concept, but it is a very important one to grasp, lest we misjudge the Servers of mankind because we see some of the limitations of the rather crude instruments They have to use. In any case, it is to be remembered that probably most of the Masters, except perhaps Those who live far away from human contact, have considerable limitations in the personality.

They are marked by two supreme qualities — wisdom and absolute dedication to the service of humanity — which result in constant subordination of Their personal interests and desires to the welfare of the work They are seeking to do.

They are bound by time and space. The resources and knowledge at Their command are distinctly limited. The strain to which They can submit Their physical bodies has a definite measure, and Their work as individuals is of necessity always secondary to the obligations of Their offices, for all of Them hold offices of greater or lesser responsibility regarding the supervision and directing of the planet upon the inner planes.

Some of the Masters are closely allied to political work, studying day and night the wisest methods to influence the leaders of the world into constructive paths. Others are closely allied to the deva work and counsel with the Shining Hosts in the distribution of forces to the planet which are at the command of the devas.

Other Masters are deeply engaged in research work which has to do with different members of the solar system, in studying how the planetary influences or extra solar system influences may be drawn to our aid and applied to problems here. Others again are concerned with the reception of visitors from diverse worlds and the museums of records in which must be kept accurate replicas of all the important inventions of every age and various political changes which influence the well-being of the planet.

Still others are studying how to bring about physical and geographical conditions which shall make possible in future ages the unfoldment of those qualities required in new races, for the constitution of the blood largely determines the powers latent in any human vehicle. This constitution is changed by food, by air, by heat or cold, by noise or silence, by the very elemental essence which the mountains and lands and oceans breathe forth, by the minerals and magnetic areas which are built into the land long before it rises from the sea, by the composition of the soil and the resultant fauna and flora which there exist.

These are, in brief, some of the activities of the Masters. It is understandable, therefore, why so few Adepts feel Themselves at liberty to take personal pupils. Those Who do take personal pupils in most cases hold some definite official position for which They must prepare Their successors; and the pupils They take are chosen with a few that from among them the most competent may be made the successor.

Again I repeat, a Master Who takes a new pupil takes upon Himself a very greatly added burden of responsibility and effort and thereby definitely limits to some extent any other work He wishes to do.

Once He has taken a pupil, until He definitely abandons him, He gives him much the same attention, solicitude, supervision and care that a mother does her only infant child, however little this may appear on the physical plane. It is a matter of constant concern to Him — and usually constant disappointment — how the candidate responds.

It is almost impossible for a Master to draw into close contact with Himself anyone with whom He has not had strong personal ties through many lives. These strong personal ties of love, devotion and service have built into the candidate certain capacities to respond harmoniously to the Master's vibration which are a prerequisite to any training.

What the Master seeks to do for the pupil is to share with him such knowledge, wisdom, power and understanding as the Master may have, and this may only be accomplished through the merging of consciousness and breaking down the barriers of the mental body through deep and devoted affection on both sides.

Yet, however much He may love His pupil and however close the tie may be, if the progress is not commensurate with the efforts expended, the Master will not be permitted to continue the relationship. He too has obligations which are paramount and to which training pupils must be secondary.

One can well understand, therefore, why those who desire to become candidates for Initiation are urged to give utmost devotion and affection to the Master Whom they seek to serve, that by their love they may prepare to open themselves to His influence and to break down that shell which surrounds the mental body so that, as far as the Master is concerned, they may learn to blend their consciousness with His.

How true indeed is the old saying, "The mind is the slayer of the Real." It is that shell of egotism and self-centredness formed about the embryonic soul when it was seeking to hold for itself one individual human body and which was its salvation at that time which now becomes its greatest barrier and menace when it seeks to expand out of the limited self into the union of the spiritual life.

Before a candidate approaches a Master and asks for training, he should realize the sacrifice that he is requiring and be prepared in turn to throw every power of willing devotion and of aspiration that he has into the task of fitting himself to make use to the fullest extent of the sacrifice that he is requiring.

CHAPTER 12
Requirements of Rays

Three Lords of the Law exist in space. The first is Master of the Elemental Forces in their original state; He hews the rock. The second is Master of Love — the light which purifies, the fire that burns away the dross. He extracts the ore. The third is the Forger of Tools, and He is the Master of the Five Rays. He directs and guides and gives to each man that form of activity which shall be his.

The seven rays represent the seven major types of force in our system.

The requirements exacted of pupils of the different rays vary somewhat, dependent probably upon the type of force handled by each ray and its effects upon the vehicles. Certainly the 1st Ray is especially exacting in its requirements, perhaps because more responsibility devolves upon it for the guidance and control of other lives.

It should be borne in mind that, although all rays work upon the physical plane, certain ones focus primarily there. These are the 1st, the 4th and the 7th. The 2nd and the 6th are especially focused in the desire world and the 3rd and 5th in the mental. Those rays which have to do with the conquest of physical matter in its densest form are necessarily very exacting in the discipline they require as regards physical action.

It is the purpose of evolution on these rays to achieve perfection of action as far as possible, perfection of constructive knowledge in form-building on the physical plane.

To that end, pupils on these rays bring all resources of mind and heart to improve their technique in action.

The teachers of the 1st Ray lay special emphasis upon truthfulness, honor, business integrity, courage, impersonality. Without these qualities strongly entrenched in the nature, a candidate is rarely considered, let alone accepted.

Those who seek to achieve Initiation upon the 1st Ray will be called upon to lead others. They have responsibility not only for their own lives but for those of many others who will follow them. It is they who will be called upon to see the Vision for building the Race by which the people must be led. It is they who will be called upon to interpret the laws suitable to each new age. It is they who stand at the threshold of the world and draw from outer space those forces needed for the progress of the race, and it is they who direct those forces upon the race for its stimulation and development.

How absolute is the necessity, therefore, that they see clearly. How absolutely necessary that they do not compromise with truth, that no latent fear, dishonesty or personal desire sway them from that undeviating line of rectitude which alone can mark the way safely for their people. It devolves upon them to lay foundation stones upon which the whole future structure of civilization is to be built, and that foundation must be strong and accurate and sound since upon it all the future must rest.

Power is achieved through rigid discipline of the vehicles so that they become at once accurate and flexible, responsive to whatever task is put to them, and yet so cleansed of elemental desire that the pupil remains utterly impersonal. This needs a very nice tempering of the three vehicles, and every latent weakness must be hammered out.

Not that an absolutely God-like human is to be created; probably as long as we live in an imperfect world where we must use the crude products of our present humanity, as long as we are bombarded by the tempests of evil and destructive thoughtforms which at present sweep our planet, the strain which the occultist puts upon his vehicles will result in certain human faults and failings even among the greatest.

Faults and failings will come not from fundamental weaknesses of the nature but will be due merely to the passing stress and strain to which the vehicles are subjected. Foibles of personal taste, nerve strain when sensitive vehicles are exposed to the noise of our civilization, temporary impatience when blocked by the stupidity of the human material which must be molded, heartsickness at the coarseness and crudity which still exist in our world, heartbreak at the cruelty and suffering which lie like an evil cloud over the progress of humanity — these may appear.

Under constant assault of such problems which the occultist can never forget — as may the average human immersed in personal pleasures — the vehicles react at times to strain like any human body, but the purpose to serve and the will to serve and the power to serve never falter.

Requirements of the 2nd and 6th Rays differ from the 1st. Here devotion, compassion and tenderness must appear in a very high degree. These two rays have to do more with training the individual than with the development of races. As in the past it has been recognized that the functions of state and church differed widely in their responsibilities, so do the duties of the rays differ.

The 1st, 4th and 7th Rays deal with humanity as a whole, with government and organization. They must follow the law of their kind that the welfare of the whole must take precedence to the welfare of the individual.

In the outer world and in many religions, in order that individual hardships which result from the law of organization and government may be mitigated, the church offers the confessional, the solace and comfort of priests to the individual, promising that confessions of the individual necessary for the relief of the anguished soul shall not come under the jurisdiction of the law which would be obliged to exact punishment.

Law must exist for the welfare of the whole, but when they repent of their sins, mercy and solace must be given sinners to prevent disintegration of the human soul. In all great civilizations these distinctions have been recognized, and the duty of the priest and the ruler, therefore, have differed so that all human needs might be met by one group or the other.

Hence, it is clear why the requirements of the 2nd and 6th Rays will be differently emphasized from the active rays. In time he who will become a Master must gain a considerable degree of all virtues, but in the beginning the emphasis will be differently placed. Tenderness, compassion, forgiveness, knowledge are required on the 2nd Ray. This ray must be not only the comforter but the teacher, not only the priest but the physician, and charity is more important than some more executive qualities.

Focused principally upon the mental plane, the 3rd and 5th Rays have in turn other requirements. They represent the intelligence aspect, in many ways more akin to the 1st in their requirements than to the 2nd. They represent science with its great impersonality; the conquest of the forces of nature, with high requirements of courage, precision and accuracy, perfection of detail, great impersonality of mind.

The 3rd and 5th Rays are concerned less with the welfare of humans as individuals than either of the other two groups. The 1st Ray must train its leaders and study the comfort and happiness of the race. The 2nd must work for the welfare of each individual soul. The 3rd and 5th Rays deal with great organizations in which achievement requires the subordination of the individual to gain the highest fruits of co-operation. Theirs is the standard of the hive where the welfare of the hive rises supreme and all individual needs are dwarfed thereby.

They it is who will ultimately govern this planet when the world shall have been organized so all people have their appointed place in the great organization which they can fill wisely and well. We see forerunners of these future rulers of the world and the organization of the world in great businesses which now exist and foreshadow that complete world organization of the future.

Then all rays existing on the planet will be subordinated to the great Third aspect of life. The 1st Ray will have served its purpose and passed on, leaving behind its organizers in the 4th and 7th. There will be no further need for priests and seers for all men will be serving the planet to the glory of God, and the 2nd Ray too will pass onward.

The reflection of the 2nd Ray will appear in the teachers and functions of personal relations courts and similar agencies in big corporations. Only the five rays (from the 3rd to the 7th) will remain in activity — in reality the only ones which belong to the three lower planes of manifestation upon which humans normally function.

CHAPTER 13
Qualifications for Initiation

When the time approaches for the Master to present the chela for Initiation, the chela must prove to the satisfaction of the Brotherhood that he is fit for power to be bestowed upon him. He must pass certain definite tests to prove the progress he has made, and before taking these tests he must weed out the faults of the personality which would prevent him from being a selfless and efficient instrument.

The qualifications are divided into four major parts. One description of them is:

1. Point of view
2. Renunciation
3. Power
4. Sacrifice

These points have been variously stated and are sometimes called Discrimination, Desirelessness, Good Conduct, Love. Perhaps they may be analyzed from another point of view in such a way as to throw added light upon the practical problem of attainment.

The ground covered earlier has brought the chela through preliminary tests. He has turned from the world and has set his foot upon the swift upward path. He has met the tests of the elementals and has not been turned from his chosen way. He has proven his devotion to the Master and his desire for service. With the knowledge he has gained he must now train and discipline his personality.

He must prove not only his desire but his capacity to succeed, and through all the hours of waking consciousness in every action of the day, he must see the opportunity to discipline his vehicles and prove his powers. The following pages seek to show in the most practical way the application of the laws of discipleship of daily life.

1. Point of View or Orientation

It has been said that the greatest gift a Master can give His pupil is a change in his point of view. As one passes through the seven ages of man from childhood to maturity, the most noticeable change is that in the point of view.

The highlights of childish joy fade as the desires of adolescence arise. The desires of adolescence make way for the ambition and mental achievement of maturity. The differences between the moron and the average man and between the average man and the leader and the leader and the Master lie largely in the differences in what each considers important in life.

Increasing discrimination between relative values — between the important and the unimportant — constitutes maturity of the soul. The Master seeks to teach the chela the point of view of the Son of God, that in the light of divine wisdom he may see life as it truly is and choose rightly between the essential and the non-essential.

Only as man understands the purpose of life and the path he must tread to divinity, only as his consciousness soars beyond the limitations of the planet and all planetary life, only as he glimpses something of the whole Plan in its vast majesty can he discriminate wisely as to actions in daily life.

The history of humanity shows that growth and civilization are marked by a gradual changing of values. Those things admired by the savage and primitive man — brute force and ruthless courage — are not the virtues most valuable and therefore most valued in the civilized man.

Not only has his environment changed, so that powers of mind are more essential than powers of body, but the old virtues have lost their significance, supplanted by more complex and intellectual concepts. Honor, truthfulness, unselfishness, sacrifice have become the virtues which have built a useful system where man curtails his own liberties for the sake of peace and good will in the group.

In like manner those virtues which belong to the man of the world must be supplanted by new virtues in the occultist. Just as the virtues of the brute, necessary to his environment, are out of place in civilized man, so the virtues of the civilized man, however necessary and valuable to him in the outer world, must often be radically modified in the occult life.

The devotion to family and friends — the keystone of our civilization — must become secondary to those virtues of the occultist: loyalty to the work and to the service of humanity. Yet, just as the brute force which has taught the primitive man to defend his own home lays the foundation for that loyalty and sacrifice for the family which marks the best type of civilized man, so the virtues of the civilized man lead directly to the more impersonal virtues of the occultist.

In no way are standards of the occultist relaxed; on the contrary they are more stringent. As in the army a soldier's first loyalty is to duty rather than to family, so the loyalty of the occultist to his work and to the welfare of humanity transcends the love and devotion he feels for his own.

Indeed, this must be so, for as he progresses in power and begins to direct and disburse the occult resources of the planet, he must be above the temptation of seeking to use them for the aggrandizement of his own, just as the disburser of public funds must be above the temptation of diverting any of these for the use of his own family.

The Brotherhood is indeed a pledged army — pledged to guard and protect the planet as far as lies in Its power from evil and destructive forces, and pledged as soldiers are pledged to put the welfare of the whole above that of any individual, however dear to them.

One can see from this how our human institutions, such as the army of defense, are preparing the way for those final great responsibilities which lie upon the shoulders of the Brotherhood and the Hierarchy. With all its horrors, war in the past has nevertheless harnessed the destructive energies of man in such a way as to do the least damage so that he gradually learned the virtues of obedience, self-sacrifice, loyalty and idealism.

Every soldier is taught and profoundly believes that he is fighting for the salvation of his people against the encroachment of a dangerous enemy. Only through struggle and conflict in the past have nations gained the discipline which they needed.

In the evolution of the planet, however, the time has come when great wars of empire can no longer serve the best good of the world. Virtues won in that terrible school must be developed by less savage and brutal means, modified and supplanted by other virtues developed through cooperation and peace.

In daily life we often see men risk their lives, and thereby the safety and well-being of their families, in some desperate venture for the service of others — the fireman in his field, the soldier, the coast guards, especially the doctors and nurses who go to tend the plague-stricken or the wounded. Is it, therefore, not suitable that he who aspires to enter the Guardian Band of the planet with its vast responsibilities and great powers should be prepared to pledge a loyalty to that service which shall take precedence to the needs of his own family in times of emergency, just as these other servers of humanity have done?

Perhaps some of those who have heard of Initiation and of the Masters and of the occult path look upon it more as a matter of personal progress, of personal illumination and increased vision. Some of these things may come, but what a candidate really does is to offer his services to the most difficult, the most dangerous, the most exacting and the most self-sacrificing task which falls to the lot of mankind.

Entering the Brotherhood entails superhuman strain, unending responsibility, constant attack from destructive forces and the constant necessity for ever-increasing discipline and selflessness of the personality. Yet throughout the ages men have leaped forward to sacrifice and service in a desperate cause, moved by the glory of ideals, disregarding comfort and pleasure, love and companionship; and so today, in spite of all the exactions, men and women are seeking to enter the Brotherhood to share Its responsibilities, Its pains and Its sacrifices.

Yet those who offer themselves as candidates would do well to remember that the exactions are heavy; that they must be ever on guard; that they must never for a moment relax their efforts to move forward to the loftier heights before them, for upon this precipitous Path one may not stand still. If one does not go forward, one slips backward, and unless one's mind is kept constantly oriented to the vision of the goal, one cannot see the Path clearly amid the dusty highways of the world.

It is the point of view of the Master — of the paramount importance of the work, of the necessity for the service to the race and of duty before which all other duties are dwarfed — which is the first requisite for the candidate for the Path of Initiation.

Be it clear that service to the world does not relieve one of personal responsibilities. When the soldier is not called upon to fight, he must fulfill the duties of his family life, the duties of the citizen, the duties of the son, father and husband. Similarly, the occultist, unless a greater duty arises clear and unmistakable, must fulfill his family obligations to the uttermost. Indeed, his family obligations within reason form part of his service to humanity — provided he does not permit any member of his family to enslave him or to determine his obligations for him.

As he protects, educates and cares for those dependent upon him, he performs a necessary part in the social scheme and therefore a part in the planetary scheme. But he must bear always in mind his occult responsibilities, that he may see his worldly duties in proper perspective. It is this necessary discrimination between the essential and the non-essential, between the greater and the lesser duty which gradually marks the growth of wisdom in the Initiate and probationer.

The goal of humanity is the development of judgment, for judgment is the flower of the creative mind. Love is the matrix within which judgment must grow, but judgment is the quality — through the unfoldment of mind — which humanity must gain. The growth of wisdom marks the progress of the soul through all the cosmic schemes, and wisdom can come only through wise judgment based on discrimination.

2. Renunciation or Desirelessness

The next great qualification is usually expressed as renunciation or desirelessness. It is the gradual tearing loose of those tentacles which hold us to the personal life, of the multitude of small personal desires which govern and make up for the most part our personality. One must lose the fear of life and the fear of death and the fear of loss of comfort. And yet, every soldier perforce practices these virtues. They are harder to achieve without that fine fire of enthusiasm which lights the soldier in his duty with the mass emotion of a great emergency.

The human tree has its roots in the ground, and it clings to the earth and feels that all the majesty of its leafy head comes from its strong grip upon the soil. And this is true. The power and success of the personal life depend a good deal upon its grip on the physical plane and upon the multitude of little desires that run out like tentacles and hook onto various aspects of physical being.

Tear these ruthlessly asunder, and the very life force of the incarnation dies. It dies into indifference, into lethargy and into death. This is what does happen at death and why so often indifference precedes death, particularly after a long illness.

Such destruction must be avoided. Those tentacles which lead to strength and power must not be torn loose until they can be reestablished above in the impersonal worlds to feed the impersonal life. Instead of drawing sustenance from the earth, they must draw sustenance from the spiritual worlds. Instead of reaching up to take, the individuality must lean down to give, and rooted in that world of divine power and love, he must find strength above to issue to those still rooted in the lower worlds.

Personal desires must be consumed by the flame of devotion. The personal life must be distilled so that it becomes spiritual essence, remembering always that without that personal life there could be no spiritual essence. As the orchid draws its sustenance from the air and seeks no contact with the rich soil of Earth, so the occultist must draw his life from the inner worlds, seeking no comfort, no sustenance, no support from the life of the personality.

We see a symbol of the occult life in the great Tree Yggdrasill of Norse mythology whose roots were deep in the heavens, whose trunk and branches touched the Earth.

In the truest sense, desirelessness means selflessness. Only as selfishness and self-centredness of the human heart are cleansed away in the Light of Spiritual Vision can the personal self render obedience to the will of the divine universal Soul where alone it can achieve divinity.

It is necessary to carry this desirelessness to a very high degree of perfection. As one clings to form, as one clings to the habits and the comfort of the body, one fails to leap forward to seize what may prove a supreme opportunity. The shot and shell of the battlefields, the danger and discomfort of wounds do not daunt the ardent soldier from volunteering for desperate service.

But it is easy in the personal life to be turned aside from an opening door to the higher life by some small complex of the lower mind which — with its small grasping desires, its preferences and dislikes — clouds the intuitive vision of the true path.

Desirelessness does not require asceticism. One should not renounce the joy in beauty, nor the capacity for love and tenderness, nor the power of affection for those near and dear. Renunciation requires freedom from the grip of the elementals so that a man may — as he thinks best — use or refrain from using any force in the body. It is not necessary to refrain from food. It is necessary only to control the appetite, that wisdom and not desire guides it.

This is true of all physical functions. The Master is a Master because He is master of Himself — not because He acts or refrains from acting in any particular way, but because He is free through conquest of Himself from the blinding of wisdom by desire. No function in the physical body has not its Godlike purpose. But undeveloped man is a pawn of Nature which guides his actions by magic spell and glamour into the channels She desires for the fulfillment of her Purposes.

Until a man is released from glamour, until he is no longer guided by passion, by wrath, by greed, by lust, he is not free. Once free, he may use or not use any of his powers — mental, emotional and physical — as wisdom directs and not be bound thereby. Asceticism is no virtue in itself except insofar as it is a means to an end to teach self-conquest. But the purpose of life is not asceticism. It is self-mastery. Therefore, the Master marries or not as best serves the purpose of the divine plan. We know the Manus must marry — not occasionally but repeatedly through many lives, that they may build the type. Marriage in itself is not incompatible with the occult path, but never must the occultist permit himself to be dominated by the elemental force, for therein lies danger.

Renunciation means complete subjugation of personal will to divine will. It means attainment of true selflessness in the service of man and God.

CHAPTER 14
Qualifications (Continued)

3. Power

The third qualification — Power — requires the development of all the force latent in the vehicles, roused, purified and directed by the divine flame of spiritual will. Only awakened spiritual fire can carry a man onward through the trials, ordeals and dangers of the Path. Indeed the spiritual will is that alone which can at last permit the lower personality to achieve divinity and conscious continuity. The Kingdom of Heaven is taken by storm, and only by the stormy power of atma reflected in the lower vehicles can the great assault be accomplished. It is hard to speak with enough emphasis of the need for this awakening. Indeed without it all else is valueless, for without it the spiritual worlds are forever sealed.

Through the power of will, intensive and penetrating as the blue-green flame of an acetylene torch, the vehicles may be purified, aligned, trained and perfected so as to become a powerful and skillful instrument for the Divine Self.

Once a man has gained some of the true points of view, once he has freed himself from the tentacles of desire, he is ready to begin the attainment of power.

It must be a beautifully trained and perfected instrument in the three worlds that he offers to the Master.

Power depends upon skill in action directed by a flaming will. The man must begin to polish and perfect all the powers of the personality. Many people aspiring to

the spiritual life tend to neglect the personality, to disregard
it, to seek to dwell in a realm of fancy far removed from the
grossness of the physical plane.

This is diametrically opposed to the plan and purpose of
evolution. We are in the three worlds of form to perfect an
instrument whereby the worlds of form and the powers
therein may be mastered. The personality — which
includes the mind, emotions and body — corresponds to
the Third Person of the Trinity, the Holy Ghost.

The Holy Ghost is the principle behind all manifestation
of form, whether it be cosmos, planet or individual, plant,
molecule or atom. We dwell today in the kingdom of the
Holy Ghost, and we dwell therein by virtue of a set of
vehicles called the personality which has been created by
the help of the Holy Ghost for the purpose of gaining
conquest over the forces latent in manifested form.

The essence of personalities never dies. Though the time
may come when the Holy Ghost and the Son are drawn into
the Father during the Night of Brahma, yet when manifestation recurs, as recur it must, the Holy Ghost will again
manifest in form. And any individual — whether human,
superhuman or divine — desiring to function in the worlds
of manifestation must use those forms which represent
the Holy Ghost in himself and which he has built with
care and endless effort in the realms of personality by
repeated incarnations.

Many of us who aspire to the vision of the higher worlds
are wont to discount and belittle the place and purpose of
the personality. When esoteric students talk of their egos
and their monads as being of consequence, it is well to
remember that these are occupied in their own spheres, that
they exist as entities only for the purpose of contacting
those spheres in which they function and are but remotely
concerned with the problems of the personality.

The personality must attain for itself, must win for
itself the conquest of its own kingdom, the worlds of
form. It is only as it succeeds in meeting successfully the

requirements and exactions of physical life here on this physical Earth that it can ultimately obtain liberation from this planet.

The purpose of incarnation in form is to develop the powers latent in form — to unfold, control and direct them. When the personality has thus mastered its own kingdom, it is ready to cooperate with its divine Master. It has fulfilled the end of the plan of incarnation and can become an effective instrument in the hands of its Higher Self for successful work in future worlds of form.

Ultimately, the worlds of form are dissolved and the essence drawn into the Universal Life, but surely not until they have reached the highest point of perfection possible in the present manifestation. We, in turn, cannot expect to be freed from the limitations of this planet until we have made of our personality an instrument so skillful and perfect that it has mastered the forces of the three lower worlds.

"Circumstances?" said Napoleon, "I must make circumstances!" So must the personality conquer the limitations of the worlds in which it dwells. Then, and then only, is it prepared to ask for release. A release from incarnation in the worlds of form can be but temporary since sooner or later a spirit will wish to use once more the powers gained in the worlds below. And then that vehicle, which it will build for that new world of form on some far distant planet or system, can comprise only those powers it has gained during its successive personalities on this planet.

Therefore, the way of power is the way of conquest, and the way of conquest is the way of discipline — the conquest, coordination and training of the three vehicles of the personality.

Under the heading of Power are six sub-headings: enthusiasm, faith, courage, skill in action, impersonality and obedience. All these are necessary to the unfoldment of the power latent in the vehicles.

It must be remembered that the purpose of the occultist differs from the purpose of the average good man of the world. With the occultist the achievement of virtue is but the preliminary step to the achievement of power. Virtue must safeguard the use of power, but virtue without power can accomplish little. In the higher worlds no man without virtue can be considered, but no man without power can be accepted.

Enthusiasm. First upon the list comes enthusiasm, perhaps one of the most gracious and divine qualities in nature and without which no soul can travel through the rocky fastness and shadowed crevasses of the Path of Initiation. It is the motive power of all endeavor, the mainspring of all effort, and without it there is no progress.

Where enthusiasm fails, life fails, and in achieving desirelessness one must be careful to guard the sacred flame of enthusiasm. It is that which replenishes courage. It is that which gives the power to rise again after repeated failure. It is that which makes it possible to take the Kingdom of Heaven by storm.

Without it the interminable training and discipline of the nature would become intolerable. Without it joy would cease, and without joy — whether it be joy in service or joy in beauty or joy in love — without joy life becomes unendurable and physical forces ebb. When we lose the joy in physical plane delights, when the normal force of the elementals has been diverted, it is only the divine fire of enthusiasm which comes from the inner worlds that gives us the strength to carry on.

Faith. Closely related to enthusiasm is faith — not a blind faith, not a narrow faith, not a dogmatic faith, but faith in the capacity to achieve divinity; faith in the ultimate beneficence of the Plan; faith in the wisdom and goodness of those inspired and loving Entities Who guard and govern our system and Who are for us perhaps best represented by the term God, by that all-embracing Tenderness and Love which watches over the destiny of Earthly man.

As man sets foot upon the rocky path of occultism, as he aspires to divine heights of achievement, he must prove himself conqueror of the destructive forces of the planet, and step by step as he goes upward, he is exposed to the assaults of various destructive forces — of wrath and fear and hatred, of despair and darkness, loneliness and doubt — in a way no ordinary man can conceive, protected as he is by the Guardian Wall the Masters and Adepts form about the schoolroom in which most humans function.

Just as the child in school cannot conceive the evil which exists in some of the more degraded spots of the Earth because he is protected by his parents and teachers, so the average man rarely contacts those destructive elemental forces which assail the candidate.

Perhaps the most terrible and destructive of forces is doubt — not doubt in any particular phase, nor in any particular plan, nor that reasonable questioning of any particular path, all of which are necessary to every step forward, but that devastating doubt closely allied to despair which makes the world seem futile and dreams of divinity hopeless and unreal.

In dark periods through which every soul must pass, where there seems no light anywhere, no help anywhere, no strength within himself, he must hold by faith, by faith and hope, until the darkness lightens. Lighten it will and must, if he truly has faith in the ultimate beneficence and wisdom of the Plan. A man may lose faith in any individual, he may lose faith in any leader and probably will. He may lose faith in any particular way or plan, but he must keep that ultimate faith that there is a Path in order that when his footsteps falter and fail, when he loses the Path, he may through faith find courage to seek and find it once more.

Every man must face the darkness, that little by little the light of his own soul may shine forth; but he will face it more successfully if he can always hold like a beacon light of the soul that faith in the beneficence of God which in time will no longer remain a matter of faith but shall become knowledge.

Courage. No man may tread the Path of Initiation without courage, that diamond quality which one sees shining so bright in the human race under adversity. One must have courage to attempt the Path. One must have courage to tread the Path. One must have courage to attain the citadel — courage to venture where the mass of humanity will not follow; courage to bear the jeers which attend the lonely seeker, courage to do right at any cost, courage to surmount those destructive forces which can be surmounted by courage alone, courage to dare and courage to do.

Courage is not recklessness. Recklessness is often motivated by fear — fear to stop and so face the danger judiciously. It is haste to action without caution or judgment. Ultimately, true courage will lead the sons of man out of the pit of error and doom into which they have fallen.

Skill in Action. These three qualities assured, as the matrix within which he can unfold his powers, the candidate turns his will to training himself in skill in action which is after all the means of conquest of the lower worlds. Skill in action means efficiency in every active department of life; without it no man may progress far in any world.

Capacity and ability are even more valuable to the Occult Hierarchy than to the business world and certainly more necessary, as greater issues are involved.

To gain capacity one must have, first, accuracy. Without the ability to receive instructions accurately and to carry them out accurately, no one may go far on any path. There must be accuracy of vision, accuracy of memory, of sight and of observation. There must be accuracy of speech and in fact all those accuracies which make a good business man, a good soldier, a good occultist.

As one progresses in the occult world, one enters a vast laboratory full of dangerous elements and destructive forces. Gradually one is trained by the chief chemist to manipulate and handle these dangerous forces. The ability to carry out instructions accurately in the tiniest detail is more essential in the occult world, therefore, than in a high power machine shop or chemical laboratory. Far greater destruction may result in the inner worlds from the failure to carry out instructions accurately than on the physical plane, although on the physical plane it may result in the death of thousands.

Next, there must be promptness. No one who has not a sense of the value of time can go far on the occult path. He who is not prompt and who thus wastes the time of others fails in this occult duty. The power to do a thing at a given time — to have necessary things ready at the appointed time, so to manipulate forces on the physical plane that engagements and agreements may be depended upon — is of value equally to the business man and to the occultist.

Another occult qualification is business rectitude or integrity. Money, although a symbol, is a symbol of something holy. It is a symbol of human labor. It is also that accumulated reserve which makes possible the gradual lift of the race from savagery, the expanding of new countries and new resources that in time all members of this troubled planet may experience comfort and well-being.

Money should be respected — not for its power to bring luxury but for its power to raise the race to those heights which shall free it from the brute labor of the past. There is a strange occult reaction to debt in any form, and the man who is solvent, and the organization who is solvent, and the nation that is solvent face the world with a courage which only solvency can evoke.

One of the great occult lessons all humans must learn is not to contract for that which they cannot pay. Debt has a corroding and suffocating effect on spiritual life and spiritual forces. Therefore, business integrity which ranks so high in the business world ranks perhaps even higher in the spiritual.

Wise administration of money comes under this head, too, for it is one of the resources of the planet, and the would-be occultist must learn to administer wisely every resource at his command, whether it be health or time or money.

I have likened occultism to business because efficiency is the keynote of business, the keynote of the great races of the future, because our coming civilizations are to be built upon the virtues which business inculcates, upon the qualities of the great Third Aspect which business represents.

There have been three great types of civilizations. One is empire built, built by warriors; one, the priest rule, built upon the religions and teachings of the priests. Now comes the third, built upon the power of organization and the training which comes through cooperation and efficiency in business which is to shape the future races.

The final quality of efficiency is tact, that skill in action, skill in speech which teaches us to work harmoniously with others, needed in all worlds. The occultist must ever be dealing with humans. He will destroy his efficiency by personal shortcomings of disposition or of understanding.

Under these various headings come the requirements of skill in action, requirements which will prepare the candidate to be of some use in the physical world and without which, however lofty his aspirations, however benevolent his intentions, he may lamentably fail.

Impersonality. Perhaps the most marked difference between the big man and the little man of the business world is the power of the big man to accept and apply criticism. No one can go far on any path who is not eager to learn. To learn one must welcome criticism and apply it.

Impersonality alone can truly value criticism, and impersonality arises from that true humility of spirit which knows its own divinity and need not pander to personal vanity.

During the earlier stages of evolution, for his protection in a world of strife, man surrounded himself with self-created glamour; otherwise he could not have endured his own crudities and deficiencies. But as man seeks to achieve, he must learn to destroy this glamour and to see himself truly, else he cannot round out his nature and attain that balance required of the Adept.

Every man has the vices of his virtues. He has the limitations of his unique line of development, and he has gone his own way for so many incarnations that there are warps in his nature which he cannot recognize. It is here that the teacher gives his greatest service for he helps the pupil destroy the glamour which blinds him and shows him incisively the weakness he must conquer.

But again only impersonality can gain full value from this service. That pride — disguising itself as mortification, as inferiority complex, as discouragement — destroys the value of the Master's counsel. Impersonality accepts criticism gladly and raises a man almost to the threshold of divinity. It is the quality which makes the unknown soldier, without which no great achievement can be won.

Obedience. Finally, as part of the achievement of power, comes the quality of obedience. No man who cannot obey can command. And the Occult Hierarchy in the Inner Worlds is based upon the law of receiving commands from our superiors and giving commands to those below you. Therefore, the power to give obedience is necessary. Probably the greatest vice which man has to fight is disobedience.

One should not be obedient to all people. One should not be at all times obedient to constituted authorities, else some of the great reforms and revolutions of the world could never have been achieved. But during the time of our training, one must give the most perfect and complete obedience to those whom we recognize as our occult teachers and leaders in all matters which relate to the training we are receiving. Later, one obeys only the Higher Self.

One may at any time disagree in opinion or policy with one's teacher, but in all matters of occult training one must either obey one's teacher or abandon him, just as one must obey one's chemical professor while experimenting in the laboratory or leave the laboratory. It is a very delicate matter of discrimination, and one is always at liberty to leave the laboratory when one loses confidence in one's professor.

But it is neither fair nor safe to continue to experiment in the professor's laboratory and disobey the instructions which he gives. Most of all one must attain the abstract power of obedience which depends upon accuracy and precision, upon intelligence and judgment so that one may grasp accurately the instructions given and carry them out faithfully.

Those who have not been trained in obedience rarely have the precision and accuracy which permits them to take instructions successfully, and those who cannot take instructions successfully cannot profit by instruction. In other words, it is useless to teach those people who have not learned to carry out instructions successfully, and this applies on all planes.

Furthermore, obedience includes the willingness to give up one's own will in all things which concern the greater good. As a candidate progresses on the path, as he makes his links with his teachers and begins to live the life of the Initiate, he must learn to hear that inner voice which is scarcely more than a shadow of feeling to protect him from error.

He must learn to check himself and listen before action and speech, however seemingly unimportant, to see whether he has the occult right to do what he plans. In time, when he finds himself about to travel on the wrong path, he will gain a curious sense of discomfort which will warn him to reconsider his plans.

He must be prepared at any moment to abandon his own plans, no matter how carefully thought out, if he gets that slight check which warns him that they are not in line with the Great Plan, and the quality of obedience to his own inner self alone can win for the candidate that power to gain the inner response as to the correctness or wisdom of his actions, that perfect submission to the will of the greater *Self* which permits the light of the divine mind at times to guide and illumine the lesser vehicle.

Lastly, through obedience only can he become the divine instrument. As he brings himself under the training of discipline so that his own vagrant desires and vagrant will are reined and checked, he at last is prepared to become the son of the Father, the obedient assistant of his Higher Self.

He never becomes the Higher Self until that far distant period when the personality must cease, but he becomes the willing cooperator in the worlds of form, the obedient servant to those rays of wisdom and guidance which fall from the chariot wheels of his Divine Self to mark the path he must follow.

4. Sacrifice

The final great quality is sometimes called love, and sometimes sacrifice — sacrifice in the sense of making all things sacred. Love in its highest sense is sacrifice, for it sanctifies all things that it touches, but in some ways the word sacrifice may be better understood if it is understood to include love. It means sanctification of life — making all things holy. It means offering every resource of mind, heart and body, of effort, of family and possessions to God and to the service of man.

Ere the occultist or the Initiate can become the Master or the Adept, he must have won, have wrested from himself the utmost treasures the personality has to offer and laid them before the Great White Throne. He must know that neither hatred nor malice nor vengeance can ever again tempt him from the service of the race.

He must **know** that no personal love, no personal tie can ever make him falter in allegiance to the highest he visions; that he is free, not from love but from that elemental urge which sweeps humans on like a rushing wind so that in the service of their beloved one, they know neither good nor evil, they know only what they call love. From this he must be free, for at all times his vision must remain unclouded in his service to mankind.

This great elemental force has been the teacher of humanity, teaching it sacrifice and unselfishness. But it has the danger that it often so seizes possession of the man or woman that they are helpless before it and, driven by their consuming passion, commit crimes against the public welfare for the sake of the one they love.

This can never be in the Master. However great His love, it must be guided always by the laws of right and justice, by the welfare of the race. The Adept must be content to ask nothing of life; He must be prepared to give. There will perhaps always be those whom He loves more tenderly than others, His own people who will follow him through the Gateway and perhaps become the component parts of a group soul of which He is the central atom.

Of these things we know little. But the wisest teachers that we know had Their favorite disciples — not that They loved the others less but that They loved the one more because They were more akin in spirit, more near that union without barriers which we shall know when we are no longer constrained by the limitations of personality.

But when at last every act, every thought, every word becomes sanctified by the spirit of love and unselfishness, by the desire to serve, by the will to follow the Light of God, then is man prepared either to carry on the work of God here or to enter other worlds to carry on His Will there. He will then have learned the lesson of the planet. He will then have conquered the desires of personality and won his divinity by sanctifying his powers to the service of God.

The sum of all this discipline which leads to power, the most valuable result of all this training in desirelessness, in orientation, in discipline and in sacrifice will be judgment. Perhaps the most comprehensive virtue that is wholly human may be summed up in the word **judgment** — because good judgment alone can make effort, service and sacrifice valuable to mankind.

It was to attain the jewel of judgment, the divine gift of creative mind, that the Sons of God began their long pilgrimage through human incarnation, and when the pupil has seen the Star of Initiation, when he has proved his knowledge of good and evil by the development of good judgment, then and then only is he ready to serve the world.

CONCLUSION
The Great Law

Throughout man's long path of ascent ever before him gleams the goal of the narrow Gateway of Liberation. Through this he must pass to gain his heritage, and when he reaches at last the snowy peaks of consciousness which mark the Adept, he will have fulfilled the purpose of human incarnations.

From these heights he will determine whether he shall go on to other realms of experience and service or turn back to help his younger brethren to achieve as he has achieved. Only on the far side of the Gateway of Initiation can man know himself. Stripped of personal desire and personal pride, he enters into the life of conscious union with The Great Law which determines the plan for all humanity.

Once he glimpses this Law, once he pledges himself to cooperate with It, he begins to gain knowledge and wisdom to help this darkened Star. Before that, all is darkness, and he cannot see how to serve for the darkness in his own mind. Only as he learns to know the truth of the purpose of life and the method of achievement — not intellectually but from true inner knowledge — can he truly help mankind. The greatest need in all of life is the change of heart from selfishness to self-sacrifice and selflessness.

Through the narrow gate of self-sacrifice, where it is stripped of all possessions, must pass the soul on its journey to fulfillment and liberation. At the gate are attendant devils who whisper of the lost pleasures he forsakes who turns his face from the world — lost joys, lost comforts, lost securities which are indeed only phantoms but which lure the mind of the unperceiving. When a man at last seeks reality, all that is impermanent must pass away from his consciousness so that he holds only to the Eternal Verities of which these phantasies are but flickering shadows sent to teach him to search for the real.

At the heart of every delight lies the germ of reality which leads man to seek the perpetuation of this delight. It is but a toy given to a child to teach him to yearn for the reality it represents, as a girl is given a doll to teach her to long for children and to love their care. So life offers us the symbols of Eternal Things but breaks them in our hands lest we believe them real. Neither love, nor joy, nor happiness, nor work can remain eternally to comfort us in this realm of the unreal lest we give our heart to the world of shadows and fail to seek the world of reality where lies our heritage.

Love unspeakable, joy unbelievable, peace unbreakable await us in the realms of God. But we must first give back all the tokens we have gathered here before we may reach upward to that which awaits us there. St. Paul said, "When a man is grown, he puts away childish things." So the soul, when it reaches its maturity, turns away from the treasures of this world, of this life, to the treasures of Eternity.

These things should be understood. First, the mark of spiritual power is not phenomena, not clairvoyance, not the Siddhis. It is radiance — a clear white light which shines about the personality like a halo. It may be sensed by those who make the effort.

Second, it is not intellect but wisdom which marks the Teacher — wisdom coming from the heart, from the under-standing of life and of human consciousness. This comes to those who *live* — more often, therefore — in the lowly. It may be sensed by those who wish, by the sense of tender understanding and sympathy for the humbler souls which radiate.

Third, there must be spiritual insight — not clairvoy-ance, which is only an extension of sight, nor clairaudience, which is an extension of hearing, but spiritual penetration — which permits a soul to see to the heart of reality, to recognize true living values and to strip others of the veils of illusion and delusion which enfold the personality.

Spiritual power desires no authority, seeks no positions, asks nothing — seeks but to light the flame within another heart, the flame of spiritual fire which burns away the personal self.

These are the marks of spiritual potency — not those that feed the desires of the personality, not those that exalt the mind, not those that manifest phenomena.

The day has come when many shall rise to speak in the name of the Rulers of the Planet. It is essential that one should learn to discern the true from the false. Nay, more. The Masters Themselves are walking today among men — unrecognized, unvalued because many times They come in simple garb and in simple form for a special work. What is the mark of masters and disciples and initiates? That they recognize only one authority, the Higher Self — "Unto thine own self be true." That they serve without hope of reward, recognition or position; that they are not diverted by criticism or personal pride and most that they carry the fire of spiritual things with them — joy, assurance, peace, compassion, power, insight.

A word on compassion. The Christ is no sentimentalist. He is a living flame, a lightning flash of white light. It is His office to withstand all evil forces — nothing can withstand His power. But destructive forces are here for a purpose, and they must fulfill that purpose. They are needed in the development of human consciousness and power. A man must win his divinity. It is not bestowed upon him.

He enters human life to risk failure and damnation to attain the crown of the creative mind. Only as he conquers evil in himself and in the elemental worlds can he achieve. He must be exposed to evil, but he must conquer.

From the throes of agony shall arise power; from the darkness shall come light; from renunciation shall come peace; and *only* through renunciation can peace come. Many are not yet ready for peace. Its very stillness, its very quiet disturbs them, for they yearn for the turbulence of emotional and astral life. The more delicate and ethereal play of consciousness which comes in music, beauty, art, poetry, friendship cannot satisfy them. Yet these are part of the gifts vouchsafed by peace.

When the soul has passed through broken and troubled waters, when pain and anguish and agony of mind and body have done their work, man is ready to turn away from turmoil at any price and seek peace. Then is he ready to enter the spiritual life, then only can he value and appreciate it. Earlier it would have been unsatisfying for heaven is not the satisfaction of the senses. On the contrary, it is the starvation of the senses and the satisfaction of the spirit.

Many young souls cannot enter Heaven consciously even after death for as yet they have no capacity for enjoyment of those things which Heaven offers. They have not unfurled the pinions of the spirit wherewith to soar into the realms of God. They are still Earthbound. For these, Earthborn Paradises are established in the astral worlds as playgrounds of the child-souls of the race.

Not here can heavenly joys be found — not here, but in that realm where man reveals his true divinity, his radiant Augoides. For this, when man shall know himself divine and display that divinity in all its brilliant panoply of spiritual power, for this alone is our long and anguished pilgrimage through aeon upon aeon of time. Evolution through grosser matter is undertaken to learn slowly to unfurl the pinions of the spirit. This end alone is worthy of achievement. This end alone brings peace. This is the goal of all humanity, the fulfillment of God's plan for man.

Know the Law. Obey it as must the servants of the Law who have pledged service to it. Greater than God, profounder than the abyss of Hell, mightier than the Suns in their courses is the Law — and before it does all creation bow.

Obey the Law. That only is demanded of the Lords of Light and those who seek to serve Their will. Inexorable, irrevocable, just, supreme, unchanging and existing in all time and space — aye and in that darkness where there is no time or space — this is the Law, the Word of the Unknown Power which rules all. Only by Its Laws may it be known. Study the Laws which are eternal and through them shall come the faint glimmer of Eternal Truth.

In all generations, in all Powers, in all Planets, in all Universes, to the Great Law, all show undying reverence. It is That for which the Masters seek. It is That which the Solar Deities seek to realize. It is That for which the whole scheme of the Universes is come into being to teach.

To the Law are all things known. By the Law are all things possible. Bend before It in profoundest reverence and submission when you glimpse Its presence for — greater than the greatest God, more terrible than the profoundest gloom, more beautiful than love, more radiant than light, more exquisite than dawn, more ethereal than perfume, more pure than the heart of a child — the Law transcends all things.

Seek for It, and if you find It, bow before Its Majesty wheresoever and howsoever It be expressed. As we learn to fulfill the Law, so do we learn to know ourselves, our universe, our work and God. So only do we achieve power, love and faith, for the Law is good.

Obey — Servants of the Law — Obey!

Introduction to *Spiritual Laws*
by Carol E. Parrish-Harra

Love and will combine to create the Law of Life that enfolds all. We struggle with human life, seeing first a glimpse of law, order and harmony and seeing also chaos, pain and confusion. Here each human develops the eyes with which to see — first the physical realities, and then the mind that sees, perceives, then knows. In good time, the spiritual eye will open, and one can see the Great Plan at work in all life.

To have such clear sight, one must comprehend spiritual law as a great science of life itself. When one finds him- or herself standing at holy moments observing life unfolding, one neither weeps nor sighs — one just knows.

The laws of life form the underpinning of human experience, remaining unknown until the journey of personality is almost finished, then emerge clearly as noble, truth-revealing substance and support.

Having loved Mary Gray's *Gateway of Liberation* for some years, it was with great delight that I located a copy of her small booklet, *Spiritual Laws*. Her rules of the evolutionary arc fit well with the guidelines Mary Gray offers for those on the Wisdom Way, so we are pleased to republish her works in one volume.

Each one who would connect the inner to the outer life must comprehend the mysteries of spiritual law. The ethics of careful steps, gentle moves, single-mindedness of purpose and clear motives combine to align the servant and the master. The thread is caught, and the weaving of outstanding lives of service begins.

"Upon this hangs the law..."

SPIRITUAL LAWS
Rules of the Evolutionary Arc
by Mary Gray

LESSON 1
The Portals of Death

Man must realize the continuity of life. Life flows on like a river. The portals of death are like locks which open to allow passage into another chamber of existence, but it is the same life moving steadily toward a goal, whatever the seeming changes in scenery.

Man should know that the change after death is not great. He does not escape problems, he does not escape life by seeking to pass the portals before his time. He but loses the opportunity given him here. In some ways, the problems are more difficult after death; conditions there prevent focusing the forces at one point as can be accomplished with form. The atmosphere is more diffuse, the concentration is less, and though form is difficult to manipulate, it nevertheless isolates the problem and confines it in such way as to make it easier to recognize and easier to solve.

Let no man long for heaven. It comes only as the reward of accomplishment upon Earth. Let men respect life and use it, for it is here that his talents are required, and as he uses them he shall find the key to the Kingdom. The purpose of life is the shaping of form that it may become the perfect instrument to manifest spiritual power. The body is indeed the Temple of God, and only through the Temple can God manifest on this plane. This is the first lesson.

LESSON 2
The Law of Karma

It is needful for mankind to recognize the law of the Day of Judgment. For every act and thought and feeling, there is a day of reckoning — not to be avoided nor evaded by any false idea that one may throw one's sins upon the shoulders of the Redeemer.

Love and faith in the Saviour open channels of power which raise a man above the level of his sins and let them fall away from his consciousness. Nay more, the outpouring of love can balance and offset the sins of feeling and even of thought. They will give man strength to sin no more and courage to atone for the past without being overwhelmed by the results of his evil-doing.

Yet the actions themselves have set into motion forces which inevitably must rebound upon the doer. This is the karmic law, or fate, which governs the physical conditions of his next life. The law of retribution and reward must be taught clearly that men may know there is justice, and no deed of good nor of evil will be overlooked in the final reckoning.

An accounting comes at the end of each life for the deeds of that life, and at great intervals like final examinations comes a reckoning of the whole series of lives in a given epoch. This judgment determines man's progress and the group with which he must work in the future. Suffering inflicted upon others takes the highest toll.

Well is it said, "Vengeance is mine, sayeth the Lord," for every human can rest assured in this present day of injustice and sorrow on Earth that the balance of justice will weigh true and atonement be exacted to the last jot and tittle of the Law. When wrong is done, it cannot be adjusted by more wrong-doing. One must have faith that the Law is good and trust in its wisdom, compassion and accuracy. The mills of the gods grind slowly, but they grind exceedingly fine. This is the second lesson.

LESSON 3
Divine Discontent

Man must know he is a Divine Spirit clothed in matter for the purposes of his training and development but never bound to this Earth nor to this form. Untrammeled by the bonds of the flesh, his spirit soars in realms of wonder and beauty such as he cannot realize in the lower mind. These celestial journeys reflect themselves in restlessness and discontent in the limited form. They rouse man to action, to strange quests, to vaulting ambition, to the search for happiness.

None of these can be satisfied here, save perhaps for a brief period, for man's kingdom is not of this Earth. He labours like a mole amid the things of Earth, unconscious still of the glory of the Sun and of the realms which are his true habitation. The currents of power which come from the Spiritual Self cause him to run in many directions, seeking he knows not what.

As he tries to slake his thirst with the rewards of Earthly life, and fails, little by little he learns to look elsewhere for true fulfillment. Thus, in time he glimpses fragments of the truth and turns to spiritual things. The path is long and arduous, and when he is unable to achieve what he desires quickly, often he turns back to the world only to find frustration here too. The Path must be trod with patience, but it must be trod; soon or late, no one can escape this necessity. No one can turn aside nor seek oblivion for as matter is indestructible, so is the spirit of man. However deep he may bury himself in matter, however much he may seek to hide from the impact of the spiritual worlds, his spirit will find him out and lash him without respite until he begins to put his feet upon the Path which leads to the goal.

No one may escape, but the longer he delays, the greater will be his suffering. There is no escape through death, through denial; there is no oblivion. The Forces which created the universe are ever active, and man cannot evade the effect of Their action. He may delay and obstruct to his own undoing, but he cannot escape the will of the spirit to force him to the heights. This is the third lesson.

LESSON 4
Will and Evolution

Man must know himself the arbiter of his own destiny. He exists in a world of law which permits him to govern the conditions by which he is surrounded — not perhaps of this life but of his future life upon the planet. With his own will or willfulness in one life, he sets into motion forces which will create not only the conditions of his future life, but the character and qualities he will have.

A man frequently blames "conditions" for failure, but these conditions he himself created in an earlier existence. For good or for evil, what we are follows the pattern we shaped in other lives.

This law at once condemns and liberates a man, according to its application. Yet, since all evolution is educational, one should not shrink from facing limitations one has helped create. By facing them, by overcoming them and by making use of the lesson involved, one may rise above the conditions and find freedom of environment in the next. Man must accept the truth of the laws of evolution and the development of the powers of the spirit through successive lives. This is the fourth lesson.

LESSON 5
The Inescapable Path

The next step is the recognition of the Path. Man lives, as it were, in a deep pit into which he has fallen and from which there is no escape without knowledge of the Path. This Path has been marked for man's ascent throughout the ages by the Great Teachers. It is long and arduous, beset by suffering and by self-sacrifice, yet no other way exists to rise from the confusion of material conditions to the worlds of spiritual fulfillment.

As millions — trampling each other in their effort to snatch security for themselves — mill in confusion through the planes of matter, slowly the forces of life drive them through the portals of the Path. Like cattle who find their escape blocked, first in one direction and then another until they pass through the narrow gates of the corral, so man is blocked and checked in his ambition until at last, perhaps reluctant and fearful, he enters the portals of the Path.

Soon or late every man must pass through the narrow gates which lead to salvation and, until he does, his suffering is great. At last, despairing, frustrated, sad, he turns away from the apples of Sodom and seeks the entrance to the ancient, holy Way which leads to the citadel of God and the achievement of his own divinity. In the end, man must turn away from the selfishness of the personal life, from its limitations and disappointments, and enter the Path which shall make him more than man and lead him to those celestial realms where lies his true kingdom. This is the fifth lesson.

LESSON 6
Control of the Physical Self

The progress of man on this Earth is governed by various conditions into which he has been thrust by taking on a physical body. The vehicles he must use are the product of a long animal evolution and have deeply buried in them the instincts and characteristics of the animal past. These belong in no way to the spirit of man but are the product of the necessity for a human form.

In the long distant past when human bodies were set apart from the animal kingdom to become coats of flesh for the spirit of man, these bodies began to progress rapidly, being changed and purified, gross passions sublimated by the spiritual nature which used them. Many believe that the assumption of physical bodies was not a necessity to the human race and that the fall of man was indeed a fall from a higher level to a lower, from the etheric level to the gross physical, symbolized by Adam's being driven out of Paradise. It was then foretold he must earn his food with the sweat of his brow and that woman should bear her children in pain. These results came from entering a physical body.

Probably, since the processes of evolution turn all things to good, something valuable will be achieved. But because man has assumed the gross physical form, it follows that he has many problems to deal with not in harmony with his spiritual nature. He is encased in a physical body, a product of evolution, with many instincts and appetites at war with spiritual evolution. These must be conquered, brought into obedience and made subservient to the spiritual will. Once controlled, this animal vehicle can then serve its spiritual master here below.

It is important for man to understand clearly the difference between his real self and the garment of flesh he wears. It will account for the conflict he often finds within himself and the need to fight desperately and even ruthlessly for the control of the lower passions. If he can see this conflict clearly and realize its full implication, if he can disassociate himself with the impulses and desires of the material form and know them for what they are, Earthborn, he will more rapidly gain control of the form he inhabits. Every child should be taught to recognize the difference between himself and his body and given a clear picture of the reason for the need for self-control. Greater is he who conquers himself than he that taketh a city. This is the sixth lesson.

LESSON 7
The Kingdoms and the Plan

The next step on the Path for man is recognition of his place in the Plan, for he is not the Plan but a part of it. Other kingdoms and other evolving groups are children of the Great Logos whom He regards with as much affection as He does man. These groups are evolving side by side with man. It is his place to cooperate with them, but neither to brutalize nor destroy them. One of these kingdoms is that of the faerie and angelic worlds. They are the guardians and protectors of living things upon the planet, the plants and the trees, the rivers and lakes and mountains. Another kingdom is that of the animals who have their own destiny apart from that of man. Some few will pass into the human kingdom, offering their bodies as vehicles for the use of evolving man. But many others will pass directly into the angelic groups, never having been domesticated. Some supply the demonic hosts who are the cleansers and destroyers of the system.

Until man learns to protect the animals and to recognize their place in the Plan, he brings upon himself fear and ill-health. He must cease useless destruction and avoid cruelty and fear in the methods of killing animals for food, for these things poison the tissues and poison man.

Unless he learns to respect the rights of others and to live harmlessly, he will suffer greatly. This applies, too, to the vegetable kingdom and the ruthless destruction of the great trees for money. These trees have a purpose and place in the Plan and should be cut with care, thinning the forests, not destroying them, for the health of the people depends upon the existence of trees and flowers. Man can only gain understanding and wisdom as he learns to apply these laws. This is the seventh lesson.

LESSON 8
The Destiny of Man

The next lesson deals with the destiny of humanity. Until man realizes the goal he is to attain, he cannot walk wisely through the paths of life. Until he raises his head among the stars where he belongs as one of the Sons of God, he cannot gain the vision that he needs to attain his goal.

He continues to creep Earthbound among his brother animals, spawned by this Earth, whose vehicles he is obliged to use. But he must know himself a younger god who has stepped down into the mire of human life to gain experience and wisdom. As he learns to know his real self, he learns also that he can rise above any limitations, Earthborn, above the sin and shame and degradation of the body, since the soul is always crystal pure and ever reflects the Light of God.

As he calls upon the Diamond Soul, he can gain the power to penetrate to distances immeasurable and to wisdom profound. Yet, as he draws down spiritual power, it must not inflate the personality. It is the spirit which is great and godlike. Only as the form with its small desires and little mind becomes obedient to the spirit can man begin to fulfill his true destiny which is to make him one of the rulers of the Cosmic Scheme. This is the eighth lesson.

LESSON 9
The Lords of Hierarchy

The government of the planet lies in the hands of a group of living men who have achieved wisdom. This is called the Hierarchy. The meetings are not held on the physical plane, but in the inner worlds, as these individuals can function consciously in all three worlds that belong to humanity. They have trodden the Path which leads from the human to the divine nature. They have completed their lessons in the school of experience, but have remained with the planet to help guide and direct it. Over them are the Lords of the Flame sent by our foster-mother, Venus, to be the rulers of humanity. These do not take physical form but remain attached to certain magnetized spots on the Earth through which they can function. These places are remote and inaccessible, far from the haunts of man.

Those who have attained wisdom are called Adepts and serve man in many varied activities. A few who make themselves available to humanity become the Masters of Wisdom because they undertake to teach knowledge of the Path and because they are prepared to take pupils who aspire to the ancient, holy Way. For the most part, these Masters do not make physical contact with their pupils but train them from the inner planes. A truly aspiring soul who is prepared to undertake the arduous training required and to give himself wholly to the service of the world will find answers from one of the Masters if he is wholly dedicated. "When the pupil is ready, the Master is waiting."

The training of the Path requires not only the ordinary virtues of the so-called good man, but scientific training of the vehicles through meditation and other specific exercises of mind and heart which gradually align the man with the forces of evolution. He learns to train the will, to still and concentrate the mind, and to control the desires, until he becomes a fit chalice for the wine of spiritual life. This training makes of man's body by slow degrees the true Temple of God through which Divinity can manifest. This is the ninth lesson.

LESSON 10
Nature Spirits to Archangels

The work of the Angelic Hosts should also be understood by man for this is a brother kingdom which works in cooperation with man. This kingdom includes the small, tiny faeries or elementals which direct the flower structure and the little beings which build the atomic forms of all things upon Earth to the great Cosmic Archangels who are messengers from the throne of God.

Unseen by most since they have only etheric bodies, they work side by side with humanity in the cultivation and care of the earth, in the growing of fruits and vegetables and in supervising the forests. Various groups or families are attached to different natural phenomena. There are the Angels of the rivers and the waterfalls, of the lakes and seas. Smaller beings are attached to brooks and running streams. Beings belong to the four elements — earth, air, fire and water. There are dwellers in the glades, in the mountains and on the seas.

Only through their help do crops mature. This is recognized in India, where it is the custom to offer thanks to those who have contributed to the preparation of grains and the supplying of food to man. A small part of everything that is eaten is set aside as a tribute to their help.

The primitive people close to the land in European countries are also aware of these little nature spirits. To bring good luck to the house they put bowls of food on the doorstep as an offering to the "good people." Ireland and Sweden especially are conscious of the existence of our brother kingdom. The Greater Beings, the Angels, are recognized in all scriptures and have played vital parts in the history of the race. The health and welfare of the planet itself and therefore of man depend upon a better understanding of this law and a conscious and willing cooperation with this other kingdom. Much healing is done through one group. To another is allotted the task of caring for children. Every mother realizes that some guardian angel protects her child from the many dangers he runs or he would not grow to manhood.

The lore of the past has been lost in the intellectual materialism of the present. Confusion, disorder and disorganization in every department have resulted. Only as man begins to obey the laws of beauty, of cleanliness and of friendliness, only as he cooperates with the beautiful Beings of the kingdom can he restore health and sanity to himself and to the Earth. This is the tenth lesson.

LESSON 11
The Animal Kingdom

The animal kingdom also has its place in the Great Plan. Between animals and man must be greater understanding and cooperation, for man must realize the animals are the children of the Earth and he in turn is the child of God. Part of the work of the animal kingdom has been the slow building of bodies that they might at last become vehicles for the Divine Spirit. Yet, there is the definite line between the animal kingdom and the human, although the long ages of evolution which lie behind the animal body are repeated in the human embryo.

As the natural inhabitants of a planet to which man has come as a visitor, they should receive kindness and understanding. Man should cherish and direct the animal kingdom as he does his domestic pets and accord them a place in the scheme of things for their own growth and development apart from him. Otherwise, the delicate adjustment of the Plan is destroyed, and warps appear which lead to suffering and pain for all the inhabitants of the Earth.

The suffering of the animals and their fear are tangible forces which leave their imprint upon the fabric of life and cast shadows over the human soul. The slaughter-houses to which the animals are driven with the smell of blood and death about them fill the animals with terror, and that terror breeds poisons in the animal itself which are absorbed by the human race through their food. This in turn begets fear and cruelty in the humans themselves and they wreak upon their innocent brothers the results of the sins of others.

It is not possible for the human race to quickly change its habits of eating, nor is it perhaps desirable, but the great increase in the eating of meat is partly accountable for the increase in brutal crimes so noticeable today. The torture of animals for medicine is leading the medical profession astray. The more sensitive bodies of the new race must seek more natural remedies, herbs, therapeutics, massage, color-healing, the use of medicinal waters and baths; a better understanding of foods. The movement toward surgery and vaccines to cure disease is too drastic and too dangerous for the higher types and other methods must be found. Furthermore, the practice of torture is weakening the moral fibre of the race. We have seen some of the results in the last war in Germany when the scientific mind stopped at nothing in its brutal curiosity.

This tendency toward brutality must be checked. Of what use to save a few more lives at the cost of increase of cruelty in the whole race? "What profiteth a man to gain the whole world and lose his own soul?" There are sacrifices to increase the length of life which the spirit of man cannot accept. For, after all, man is a spiritual being and the death of one body of no great consequence. For his own sake, man must protect the animals from exploitation if he is to save his own soul. This is the eleventh lesson.

LESSON 12
The Divinity of Man

Mankind is one of the Hosts of the Lord. He has his appointed place in the circle of his brethren, and the work of the Solar System cannot be completed until he is able to fulfill his part. The Hosts of the Lord are like a strong army composed of those who march side by side, an honor guard for the Radiant One who is our God, who obey orders and carry out their instructions in the farthermost parts of the System. Only as man learns to obey and cooperate with God can the good which is intended be made manifest here.

Man has been milled fine between the grinding stones of fate. Like the Prodigal Son, he is ready now to leave the husks upon which he feeds — like the beasts of the fields — and return to his Father's house from which he has been long absent. There will be rejoicing in Heaven and glory and honour and welcome when the prodigal returns. This is the last lesson.

Glossary
by Carol E. Parrish-Harra

ADEPT. An occult degree or Soul-realized being working on laws of inner reality. Divided into two classes: one to demonstrate outward use of inner forces in human life and consciousness; the other to create reservoirs of energy to sustain forces of nature, direction of elementals, etc., to support outer manifestation.

AEONIC DAMNATION. The condemnation attributed to the wrath of God in scriptures.

AKASHIC RECORDS. Record of events and emotions imprinted on etheric level and held as memory of all planetary life. The etheric level records or reflects a living chronicle of life, the story of the planetary being, all planetary life.

ANGELS. Also known as devic evolution, an analogous family evolving parallel to humanity upon planet Earth, the densest level they inhabit being the astral. The Christ is teacher of angels and humanity, with similar levels of initiation. Angels are celestial rulers of Aquarius; Mother Mary is a master, advanced one, in this family.

ARCHETYPAL LOGOS. A great being supervising the divine Plan for a given group of solar systems. He holds the Plan while other Logoi bring it into manifestation at their levels of command.

ARCHETYPAL WORLD. The great reservoir of archetypal energies held in abeyance from which are drawn creative ideas and forces on every level. In Kabalistic thought, Atziluth.

ARHAT. Wise ones whose work now (having received the fourth initiation) is in preparation for next level. Purification of the nature of human traits is primary, pain a principal tool until will aligns to higher influences. This stage is to advanced initiations as probationer is to first human initiation.

"AS ABOVE, SO BELOW." The Hermetic Principle of Correspondence, one of seven principles underlying the laws of creation. (*See* LAW.)

ASTRAL. Sensitive ethers that preserve a living record in feeling, picture, sound and color of the happenings of all planet life. Literally translated "starry" for activity and "bursts" of activity that collect in this sensitive, feeling level of being. The combined emotional state of humanity forms a globe-encircling, -penetrating cloud, or aura, which constitutes a world of its own — the astral dimension. Attraction, repulsion, metamorphosis and transformation are dominant laws of this desire world which accommodates numerous beings who operate in diverse subtle ways, influencing humanity through desires and emotions.

ATLANTIS. A prehistoric period in human life held subconsciously in planetary and human memory; primarily a level of development called "fourth root race" where the mental plane unfolded, having emerged from the emotional (astral) plane. The place of battle between forces labeled "dark" and "light." A testing time where self-destruction reigned and humanity was found lacking, thus the remnant entered a new cycle of evolution.

ATMA. Will of highest level, or atmic plane, drawn as one can into personality to cleanse and purify one's life, aligning with higher will. In Hinduism the Self is called "Atman."

AWAKENING, THE. Secondary influence of human nature that stirs and becomes conscious of a path to high consciousness.

BAPTISM. Ritual invoking spiritual forces and guardian presence to assist one during life's challenges. This ritual strengthens the sheath of spiritual energy about one, calling for a guardian from Spirit and from the human side. Both guardians have a spiritual relationship to that one whom they serve.

BLOOD OF THE HEART. This symbol of outer life stands for personality desires; represents the grief and suffering through which it frees itself of desire domination.

BODHISATTVA. Sanskrit for one who carries Buddhic energy and in a future incarnation will become a Buddha (enlightened to Nirvana), or one whose consciousness has become enlightened intelligence, or *buddhi*. Used much like Western spiritual traditions use "Christed." In the East the office presently occupied by the Lord Maitreya, known in the Occident as the Christ. This office is that of world teacher, head of all religions of the world, master of masters and teacher of angels and of humanity. The Bodhisattva is the exponent of Ray 2 force.

BOEHME, JACOB. A mystic and simple cobbler of the medieval period (1575-1624), his writings have encouraged modern mystics in their quest. As a youth Boehme, a rural German born of peasant stock, had the ability to enter alternate states of consciousness and see into the astral light. Having learned to read and write, he was apprenticed as a shoemaker. One day he was approached by a man under extraordinary circumstances and told he would lead a life of hardship and poverty. Soon he began to have visions of extended duration which gradually became clearer. He had his last visions in 1610 and began to write about them in 1612. His writing often contains alchemical imagery, but he was a Christian mystic, hounded and persecuted by Christian authorities throughout his life. He advocated an esoteric, cosmic understanding of Christ and maintained no one needed assistance of any church organization to find fulfillment in Christ. His writings were numerous, but *The Way to Christ* is his most famous.

BROTHERHOOD, THE. The hierarchy of "elder brothers before the throne," as called in Christian tradition; saints and holy ones who have emerged from the human condition into greater oneness with the Christ. Having passed certain tests at first initiation, one is deemed worthy of the attention of the brotherhood (or hierarchy).

BUDDHI. The love of the spiritualized heart, spiritual wisdom or compassion useful in softening the destructive mind. Often refers to the energy of heart and mind blended and balanced.

CHAPELS OF SILENCE. Initial point of specialized training behind the veil of sleep, one is admitted only after some advancement has been gained. Here one is exposed to currents, archetypal energies and other stimuli to awaken inner forces, thus assisting one deemed ready to advance more rapidly in their tests and inner knowledge.

CHELA. Dedicated pupil of a guru; literal translation, servant, i.e., handmaiden or servant of the Lord.

CHRIST, THE. Head of hierarchy, teacher of angels and of humanity. The primary position of power for planet Earth, this living flame guides all life in this sphere of evolution.

CHRISTHOOD, BUDDHAHOOD. One office among many within the hierarchy of Earth.

CHRIST LIGHT, CHRIST-WITHIN. Divine nature incarnate within a human being. The illumination that emanates from and is experienced by one who perceives and receives energies of the divine Source. The love-wisdom aspect of the unfolding divine spirit within humanity, this divine life of the Logos forms the garment of the soul in each person. The Christ principle resides in every human heart — to be formed in each of us. This Immanent Spirit can never die but continues to develop throughout evolution until it is fully expressed in each human life.

CONSCIOUSNESS. From two Latin roots, *com* and *scire,* meaning "with knowledge." A state of focused awareness — the level and core of which are directly related to the scope of one's attunement to simultaneous processes of life. A registration and response to any impression, through light of the human intellect, operating on the mental plane. Consciousness expands as one's intelligence operates on higher levels, with subtler substance and within larger fields. The mind gradually assimilates and reflects light and changes into light. Consciousness is not intellect, rather the result of interaction between intellect and matter — a lighted area in which things are perceived, seen and sensed; it is created when the intellect of the soul hits matter. While intellect is the positive pole and matter (etheric, physical, astral and mental) is the negative, consciousness is the lighted area created by their contact.

DELUSION. A veil of distortion existing in the astral nature that blinds human beings to their real nature. The unreal through which one must pierce to perceive greater values life holds.

DEVACHAN. The heaven world where weary souls rest, refresh the spirit and experience no pain.

DEVAS. Also called "angels," these comprise a parallel evolution to humanity and often interact. Devic forces, often called the "builders of form," command many forces of nature. They work with the lesser kingdoms evolving on Earth and cowork nicely with humans of stable temperament, advanced in understanding spiritual law. Devas usually guide the work of elementals, serving humanity and more advanced angels on a line of hierarchical advancement. Much work has been effected to counterbalance man's destruction of 5000 years of unconsciousness. Now this force must be invoked consciously by human beings advanced enough to use respectfully and wisely the creative fires they summon.

DEVILS. Negative influences, or dugpas, that lie waiting within personality to be confronted. When faced with positive force also available, these negative aspects of self create power to meet temptation and overcome negative traits, intelligences or influences.

DHARMA. Duty, service to the Plan, to God, to Planetary Logos.

DISCIPLE. In esoteric tradition, specifically a third degree initiate; in common usage, a pupil or follower who helps spread a master's teachings. One who follows a particular discipline according to a prescribed pattern. One who subscribes to a constant habit of spiritual living and whose knowledge, capacities and spiritual abilities are demonstrated in daily life.

DUGPAS. Testing agents residing within the ego that resist light and seek to slow one on the path. The symbology of a good and bad angel represents challenges presented by devas of light and dugpas — dark elementals of self-service that must be aligned to the soul purpose before advancement on initiatory path can occur. Often called "evil" because dugpas work on the path of involution, rather than evolution.

EARTHBORN PARADISES. Those not yet mature enough to enjoy the heavens of the inner world need places in nonphysical dimensions in which to abide until they evolve into states of inner life that will have meaning. Playgrounds for young or immature souls unprepared for spiritual training.

EGO. Individualized self-consciousness; the perfect self that experiences in form and animates the will of human life; the developing, unfolding human soul. This reincarnating self is the monadic vehicle on the plane of abstract intellect, storing knowledge and experiences of all incarnations.

ELDER BROTHERS. Those who have reached heights of consciousness by traveling the path of humanity. These holy ones guide and guard those evolving by the same route, assisting them to become wise, preparing them for tests ahead — "divine parenting," we might call their service.

ELEMENTAL FORCES. Basic building blocks of earth, air, water, fire used in creation and maintenance of the physical world. These forces have particular roles; forces behind the outer form evolve through guiding that interplay. Wise Ones work through a hierarchy of responsibility constructed to allow growth at every level.

ELEMENTAL WORLD. Patterns of lower evolution are everywhere about and within the personality waiting to be confronted by the purification process. These energies of body, emotion and mind are maintained by the combined work of elementals who will be acted upon by the evolving consciousness.

ELEMENTALS OF NATURE. The guiding awareness of each groupmind forming the natural (or nature) forces of earth, air, water and fire.

ESOTERIC. The Greek root *eso-* means "within." That which is hidden, unseen or secret. An inner, or out-of-sight, process; obscure teachings meaningful to those prepared spiritually to receive them. In the New Testament Jesus spoke of teachings he reserved only for disciples and did not offer the public. His exoteric, or public, teachings were parables which, though commonly understood, also contained some deeper

EVIL. Opposite pole of good — negative and positive — is involutionary and only considered evil when on the evolutionary arc upon which one rises out of the world of matter. That which hinders soul purpose.

EVOLUTION. The progressive march toward a higher life. The natural, unfolding development of latent potential within all life, guided by an inherent design. The process of liberation of spirit from the prison of form. For humanity, the process of awakening to the plan and purpose of God, expanding in consciousness and attaining, stage by stage, an ever more inclusive awareness. (Evolution of the planet is uniquely linked to human evolution as humanity is the *manas,* or mind, for planetary life. Planet Earth evolves as value systems of planet life sensitize to purposes of the Logos.)

EXPANDING VEHICLES. Vehicles of consciousness — means of knowing — hold a line of tension between two poles (spirit and matter). As one gains more mastery of the abilities of each vehicle, it is brought under control, tested and found valuable to this evolving soul — latent ability brought to useful expression.

EXPANSION OF CONSCIOUSNESS. Progression of consciousness from one level to another as one's awareness of personal and planetary purpose increases. Ability to function effectively on more advanced planes of being or from higher states of consciousness. Registration and assimilation of energies that allow one to build new relationships and to extend one's fields of perception and activity.

GOD-WITHIN. The divine spark confined within matter which in time evolving ones realize and place in the position of honor and to whom total allegiance is given.

GODHOOD. A name given by the Christ to the exalted state that beckons all of humanity with, "Remember, thou art Gods?" State of divinity by which our creative nature is expressed and aligned to the creator of all life. "Made in the image and likeness," it is our true nature as well.

GROUP SOUL. Those whose unique qualities come together to form components of a group action around a leader, a central atom.

GUARDIAN ANGEL. Protective presence invoked by spiritual ritual to strengthen the soul as it meets challenges of human incarnation.

GUARDIAN BAND OF THE PLANET. Hierarchy of the Planetary Logos with an emphasis on service it renders that guide one.

GUNAS. Three types of force pervading all levels of creation: action (will), stability (inertia), rhythm (harmony); also known as rajas/neutral/compulsive, sattva/positive/elevating and tamas/negative/inertia.

HIERARCHY. Holy Ones who demonstrate leadership and service, awakening humanity to its greater potential and demonstrating for those aware of hierarchy a path of ascent to higher realities of life. Consisting of many departments, different qualifications, branches of the Plan, this inner structure holds the blueprint for humanity as, one by one, personalities come to know themselves as one great soul, the human soul incarnated in the world of matter.

HIGH SELF. The ball of wisdom, or sum total of awareness, an evolving soul gleans through personal experiences in this and all previous incarnations. This ball of knowledge serves as a high point in consciousness, guiding personality as it experiences life within the limited awareness of physical form.

HOLY GHOST. Older terminology for the etheric intelligence held in each level of ethers. The clear, reflective ether holds the blueprint, and other levels hold the consciousness that expresses through personality. This forms the shadow side of the divine — God in matter — and will exist until all is drawn back into rest.

HOLY SPIRIT. Third person of the Trinity; the power of active intelligence in the universe. An aspect of divine consciousness that expresses in the physical realm without physical form through overshadowing those who are receptive as a soul to this high frequency or intelligence. The aspect of divine nature that is the vital, form-building energy ensouling all matter. Generally considered to be feminine. The divine-within that delivers creative expression from the world of spirit to the world of form — the Mahat. (Also known as Christ-Consciousness, the Comforter, Holy Breath and Holy Ghost.)

ILLUSION. Maya, a veil of distortion that exists individually and collectively for humanity to ultimately clear. Also one of the original definitions for "sin."

INITIATE. From Latin root meaning "first principles of any science." One dedicated to the study and mastery of the mysteries of the science of self, the One Self in all selves. One who has made him- or herself ready to enter upon the Path of Initiation, culmination of the path of human evolution — in most Western systems divided into five steps called "initiations." In the esoteric Christian path, these steps are modeled in the life of Jesus, the Christ, as 1) birth, 2) baptism, 3) transfiguration, 4) crucifixion-resurrection, 5) ascension. Before first initiation, one is an aspirant or candidate and on the probationary path.

INITIATION. Process of awakening to one's true identity by passing through various stages of development requiring service to humanity and expansion of consciousness. Also, admission into sacred teachings or organizations of an esoteric or occult discipline; entrance into the spiritual life.

INNER PLANE CLASSES. Gatherings behind the veil of sleep to which aspiring ones can be called during sleep and out-of-body to assist and hasten evolution of consciousness. Also called Halls of Learning, where ideas and concepts are introduced, or Chapels of Silence, where energies, forces or influences are rendered. Gatherings are most often called "classes," regardless of the type of exposure that takes place.

INNER PLANES. Higher or hidden frequencies of each plane not recognized while conscious in the physical, awakened state, i.e., an inner plane experience refers to an event occurring out of sight and most often behind the veil of sleep — revealed in a somewhat dreamlike manner but not a product of the subconscious; not a dream but an experience of another dimension imprinted on the memory in a delicate or gossamer awareness.

INNER WORLDS. A realm of realities not recognized by the analytical, outer mental state.

INTER-SOLAR GROUP. Inter-cosmic forces helping the evolution of Planetary Logos, playing a role in balancing advancement toward the goal of the greater whole.

INTUITION. Direct or spiritual perception. Spiritual intellect; insight by the soul's intellect from the mind of Reality itself, beyond the domain of pure reason. A knowing or awareness at a level of mind or consciousness beyond mental reasoning or normal intellectual comprehension.

INVOLUTION PERIOD. A stage or process preceding evolution in which spirit or life descends into matter — also called "path of descent." Involution of spirit into matter happens so form may be built, making possible its evolution. Descent into matter typically is represented by a series of planets in which the least physical form is a mental globe, a thoughtform in the mind of God; then an astral form, made of the feeling or reflective ethers; then an etheric model, firmer than the previous forms; and finally the physical model, vibrating as matter, the most densely concentrated form.

KALI-YUGA. The period of planetary purification now in progress.

KAMA. Emotion.

KAMA MANAS. Mind colored by desire (ambition/personal love, masculine/feminine — equally selfish).

KARMA. Literally, "action" or "work." The total of all of one's actions, both presently and in previous lives. Also, the law of ethical causation, or cause and effect, the spiritual law wherein one eventually experiences the consequences of all of one's actions — positive and negative. This universal law insures justice for each soul as it experiences creation. As consciousness evolves, karma requires adjustment and/or compensation for all "pluses" and "minuses" — individual, group and planetary.

KARMIC DEBT. That which is due as a result of previous actions.

KARMIC SHEET. The record of cause and effect already in place.

KEYNOTE. One's fundamental response to life, determined by ray and sub-ray.

KRIYASHAKTI. The creative power ("made in the image and likeness of God") used in forming all creation.

KUMARAS. Guardians of the power of planets; arbiters of nations and continents; judges of good and evil, they form an Inner Council of Power, rendering balance of forces as needed for planetary evolution.

KUNDALINI. The primal energy of the universe — some part of which lies coiled in potential form at the base of the human spine that, when channeled upward through the body to the brain, is associated with the state of enlightenment. As this powerful spiritual energy awakens from dormancy, it rises along the spine activating the chakras, igniting change, stimulating life activity. The awakening of this mystical force is related closely to the process of spiritual evolution which leads toward final union with the Divine, or God-Realization.

KURUKSHETRA. The battleground, burning ground, a point of friction between personality and spirit for transmuting forces and forging new awareness. A second major stage occurs as the arhat completes burning ties to the human condition.

LAW, THE. The basic laws, generally enumerated as seven, are most commonly called the Hermetic Tradition — collective influences that guide all life in its evolving consciousness and through its processes of creation, order and destruction, ever imprinting the law of justice into humanity. Within this framework numerous operations of cause and effect have been defined. Hermes' seven great laws are the Principles of 1) Mentalism, 2) Correspondence, 3) Vibration, 4) Polarity, 5) Rhythm, 6) Cause and Effect, 7) Gender.

LODGE. The organized hierarchy of humanity, also called "White Lodge."

LOGOS. The supreme creator.

LORDS OF COMPASSION. Advanced ones in whom buddhi of the heart is activated. These Lords lead humanity toward super-human evolution.

LORDS OF FLAME. These exalted beings of love, light and spiritual power inspire humanity in its journey to higher consciousness, to self-mastery. With their assistance we can comprehend our inherent capacities for these aspects and responsibly apply them in our lives.

LORDS OF THE LAW. The three guides of Created Worlds: the Manu, the Bodhisattva and the Mahachohan.

MACROCOSM. The great universe or cosmos; the big picture or magnificent view of life from a cosmic perspective. A system that reflects one of its components on a large scale, e.g., the cosmos reflects the life of humanity; humanity reflects the life of a single person; a single human life represents the life of a single cell — only functioning on a larger scale.

MAHACHOHAN. Chohan of the Third Ray — Active Intelligence — assumes responsibility for developing a great civilization. Under this influence fall the masters and work of the third, fourth, fifth, sixth and seventh rays.

MAHAT. Holy Spirit, that spiritual power which initiates creative activity.

MANAS. A sanskrit word meaning "to think," refers to the mind-principle of the human. That which distinguishes human from lower kingdoms: reasoning faculty, intelligence, under-standing, individual mind, powers of attention and choice. Humanity is to evolve the mind for the planet. *Kama manas* refers to lower mind.

MANU. Founder of a great plan and builder of a root race, continents, flora, civilizations and nations; guides the work of the Bodhisattva and the Mahachohan.

MASTER. One who has developed high consciousness and lives in oneness with both God and humanity. Called "master" because he or she takes pupils and guides their personal development by sharing with them their energy and wisdom. In the Western esoteric tradition, a fifth degree initiate — one who has achieved self-mastery, thus making personality a vehicle to express the higher nature. Eastern tradition refers to the third initiation as "master." The lives of many masters give guidance to humanity.

MENTAL BODY. Layers of mind built of frequencies, each containing a record in thought established as the soul evolved. The mental body is reworked, synthesized and integrated with the buddhi as awareness expands.

MICROCOSM. The little universe, or man, manifesting in and through his physical body. Minute bits of consciousness that live, work and express within this miniature universe; acknowledging the smallest particles in the processes of life — seemingly microscopic — and the parts they play.

"MIND IS THE SLAYER OF THE REAL." Rigidity of mind can resist truth and awareness and hold one in bondage, not permitting true Reality to be perceived.

MONAD. An indivisible and divine spiritual life-atom; the immortal self within each person which lives on in successive incarnations, progressing to the stature of the Adept beyond which extends unlimited evolution. The spark of divine life, that highest part of the constitution of beings. The innermost self, the source of life and light that nurtures the unfolding soul. This true self, a breath of the Absolute, is in no way influenced by conditional, finite existence. The immortal and eternal principle within us — an **indivisible** part of the integral whole — the Universal Spirit from which it emanates and into which it is absorbed at the end of the cycle.

MONEY. Concretized energy, its value to be used with discrimination.

MOTHER PRINCIPLE. A cosmic force that leavens and nurtures.

NEW AGE. Refers less to a time period than to a state of consciousness. The new awakening consciousness expressed through thoughts and actions reflecting an awareness of the Plan and realization of the divinity and oneness of humanity and all of life. A shift in consciousness characterized by a global perspective and attention to universal questions and problems. Unity, synthesis, intellectual development, scientific discovery and ethical or spiritual living are keynotes of the present new era. Often specifically refers to the Age of Aquarius presently upon us.

NIGHT OF BRAHMA. Pralaya, a time period of unmanifest when the Second and Third Persons of the Trinity rest in the First before a renewed cycle begins.

NIRMANAKAYA CLASS. Advanced ones working with all evolving life from spirit rather than form side of life; related to wisdom, energies and influences behind the manifested side of life.

OCCULT. Latin, meaning "to conceal." The word is formed with the prefix *oc* which means "reversely, inversely, opposite and against" in Latin. It is the opposite of "cult" because its philosophy teaches one to do his or her "own thing." Occult studies were hidden, unknown to most of humanity; the science of life or universal nature. The true study of occultism penetrates deeply into the causal mystery of being, our inner orientation to God. It not only includes the physical, psychic, mental and spiritual levels of the human being, but studies the structure, operation, origin and destiny of the cosmos — also called the Hermetic and esoteric sciences. The occult was known as Kabalah in the West and mysticism, magic and yoga in the East. Studies include esoteric psychology; magic (both black and white); making contact with masters, spacials and devas; and trance work, including mediumship. Those on the path are expected to realize dedication, purification, discipline, teaching and service. As a precaution, the teachings were hidden from the selfish — educated and uneducated — so these divine sciences would not be misused or turned into black magic.

OCCULT MEMORY. That which is held in subconscious — out of sight and out of mind — of either an individual or group, i.e., humanity.

OCCULT PATH. A way of inner embracing; intense purification of the nature.

OCCULT TRUTH. Realities that lie behind the apparent and are comprehended gradually as one continues to see the "cause" side of life.

OCCULTIST. One who studies the mystery (concealed, mystic) side of life.

OFFICIALS OF THE SEVEN RAYS. The chohans and masters who exemplify the qualities of the rays and guide the seven streams of divine energy flowing from the Godhead.

OUTER PLANES. The so-called physical, astral (emotional) and mental planes of personality.

PAST LIFE. Previous incarnation on the physical dimension.

PATH. A way, a walk or journey, usually denoting the spiritual story of one's advancement.

PATH OF INITIATION. The avenue taken by one seeking knowledge of the divine mysteries of life; the process of enlightenment through dedicated service and self-mastery, and the steps or stages delineated by various esoteric systems. As distinguished from the probationary path or the path of discipleship, a higher stage of spiritual evolution. Entrance upon the Path of Initiation is marked by simplification of the life, increased self-mastery and conscious service to the divine Plan. Stages of development in which the center of consciousness is transferred from purely human awareness to early stages of spiritual awareness. Pattern of advancement. The Christian Path of Initiation comprises five great steps as modeled by Master Jesus in his life. Each step symbolizes a test one must pass and strengths one must embody to advance. (*See* INITIATE.)

PATH OF OCCULTISM. "The taking of heaven by storm" and intent, rather than comfortably awaiting advancement by evolution with one's peers.

PHILOSOPHER'S STONE. Energies, concepts and realizations synthesized and concretized by one on the path of rapid ascent, used to evaluate life experiences. This stone was the goal of alchemical art practiced in the Middle Ages. It was said a small tincture of it would transmute large amounts of base metals into gold, heal deadly wounds and completely transform the body and soul of the alchemist who achieved its manufacture. The stone is generally believed to be an allegorical interpretation of the highest states of mystical awareness attained by the alchemists as they projected their own personal transmutation process onto their chemical operations. Although the actual relationship between consciousness and matter is still a scientific uncertainty, in esoteric and mystical circles it is generally accepted that matter is just a lower vibration of spiritual modalities, therefore subject to transmutation.

PLAN. The blueprint of evolution, as made known through the Elder Brothers of Humanity. The divine Plan represents God's design for humanity, for the planet and for all life. Knowledge of this Plan can guide humanity back to the source of life and enables one to become a conscious coworker. Considered a mandala of action projected to humanity to aid us in finding our way home. A manifestation of divine law; the order and purpose that prevails throughout all existence.

PLANES (PHYSICAL, MENTAL, EMOTIONAL, INTUITIONAL). A gathering of similar vibrations and nature into defined frequencies. Each plane consists of seven levels and gradually is delineated as the dense forms a layer and the less dense builds upon it until seven substrata are formed.

PLANETARY BODY. Each kingdom forms a part of planetary building blocks. Spiritual teachings suggest humanity forms the cerebro-spinal nature of our planet.

PLANETARY SPIRIT. The vital essence (not form) energizing the life of the planet.

PLANETARY WORKERS. Those whose allegiance is pledged to the advancement of planetary goals.

PORTAL OF INITIATION. Doorway to the testing experience.

PRANA. The sanskrit word for "breath." In mystic and occult philosophy the vital air, the life principle. The psycho-electrical field that manifests in the individual as vitality. The life-atoms of the prana, or psycho-electrical field, return to natural pranic reservoirs of the planet at the time of death. Also known as *ki* or *chi*, prana is the cosmic life force on all planes of being; the "breath of life."

PROBATIONARY PATH. A time before acceptance into initiatory process when one is closely guided, tested and evaluated for eligibility for conscious evolution.

PROMETHEUS. One of the giants in Greek mythology who survived the fall of Atlantis and was a friend to humanity. Chosen to arbitrate apportionment of a slaughtered bull, Prometheus tricked Zeus into taking the bones and fat (which thereafter always remained the gods' portion) and leaving the meat for humanity. An angered Zeus withheld fire from humanity so they would have to eat their meat raw. When Prometheus, aided by Athene, stole fire from the chariot of the Sun and gave it to humanity, Zeus punished him by chaining him to a pillar in the Caucasian mountains. Each day a vulture came and ate out his liver; and each night the liver grew back, only to be eaten again. Prometheus is a symbol of the consequences incurred when humanity evolved into Self-consciousness (the fire of the Gods emits the light of consciousness). No longer in blissful preconscious slumber, humanity is now chained (by its own awareness) to the rock of materiality and must constantly undergo pains of purification (the liver is the organ of purification) in order to remain worthy of the inner fiery presence.

RAY. One of seven streams of force or emanations of the Logos; the seven qualities of God expressing individualized attributes. Each bequeaths its quality, color and sound as it impacts consciousness. The seven rays are divided into three major rays of aspect: will, or power; love-wisdom; intelligent activity, or adaptability; and four minor rays of attribute: harmony; exactness or science; devotion or idealism; ritual, orderliness or economy. Also known as Seven Spirits, or Elder Brothers before the Throne, or Seven Great Rishis in Eastern thought.

Root race. In esoteric terminology seven stages of human development during the cycle of planetary existence. As Earth's humanity passes through these seven root races, the human lifestream evolves. These progressive epochs of dominant cultural complexes, or peoples, are centered in geographic areas where the stream of divine sparks converges into expression — a root race. According to esoteric tradition, the seven primary groups in order are Adamic, Hyperborean, Lemurian, Atlantean, Aryan and two yet to emerge (the sixth has been named Aurorean). Each root race — divided into seven periods, or sub-races — attains to a climax of achievement about its mid-point, the 4th sub-race. Here a racial cataclysm begins while a new race is born of the fifth sub-race of the root race in decline. The new root race then evolves with the latter half of the preceding mother-race.

Sacrifice. Making sacred every aspect of one's life; sanctification brought about by the fire of purification as it consumes all that is not of the true self.

Salvation. Mastery of one's spirit, awakening Godhood, enlightenment. The Self-within illumines life with the light of spirit (monad).

Second Person of Trinity. The Christ, reflection of the divine Father and Mother in the lower worlds. Great Lord Christ exists as planetary guide to the source for our planetary stream of life, and the Christ-Within, or Mystical Christ, is the reflection for individual lives.

Seven Great Officials of the Rays. Chohans who distribute the force of each ray, using many sub-departments and offices.

Siddhis. The variety of ways that attest to spiritual compatibility or results from spiritual disciplines; not spiritual in their own nature.

Solar deities. "Heavenly Man," or deity, embodied in a solar system, also advancing through the expanded consciousness of each planet within one's system of which planets are centers of awareness. Our heavenly being contains all of our planets, and the Sun is the heart.

SONS OF GOD. A way of speaking of sparks of God that descend to embody and learn through experience within matter.

SOUL. The expanding spark of divinity within all life. The human being's contact with the universal source, linking human personality to monad and reflecting monadic presence to developing personality. As awareness increases, the mature human soul becomes less reflection and more the monad itself, a spark of the One Flame imprisoned within form. The life aspect which gives each being, life or consciousness the vital factor. Some use "Soul" to designate one who, having enhanced and deepened control of the soul over lower aspects, has achieved first initiation — birth of Christ-Within. Others reserve the right to capitalize Soul for the fourth initiation when it is said that one lives as a Soul or Adept. The soul is considered feminine in nature, as it births the inner Christ.

SPIRITUAL MESSENGERS. Those who descend to the outer world bringing a specific "word," a message or work to be delivered to outer reality.

SPIRITUAL TEACHER. One more-wise, little or great, who shares with others what s/he has *realized* in order to give comfort and assurance as to goals, to mark the route of spiritual conquest for others.

SPIRITUAL WILL. The will of soul or spirit within self to which one seeks to blend personality will, that the higher might be expressed.

SUB-RAY (or sub-plane). The influence of a ray expressing behind or within the cycle of a dominant ray.

SURVIVAL OF THE FITTEST, LAW OF. That which can best cope continues; all other is swept away.

THEOSOPHY. The revealed teachings given by Madame Blavatsky.

UNCONSCIOUS DARKNESS. A state of evolution where one is guided by involution, or instinctual nature; Kali Yuga is the period of purification of this level of planetary life.

VEHICLE. In esoteric terminology, "body." The vehicle of mind expresses thought; the astral (emotion) vehicle expresses feeling; the physical vehicle expresses action.

VOW OF POVERTY. The spiritual meaning: "Gives all and expects nothing."

WHITE LODGE. The hierarchy, or brotherhood, of elders leading humanity in evolution.

WISE GUARDIANS. Those from inner worlds who watch human progress, guiding and guarding as they can without interfering with humanity's free will.

WISE ONES. A common title implying those trained in the wisdom of the esoteric; certain masters, saints and sages in the Western tradition and gurus in the East. High initiates who step down the scheme of evolution to less evolved.

POSTSCRIPT
A Contemporary Mystery School
Prepares World Servers

Your role in the Aquarian Age

The decade of the 1990s is one of personal and planetary struggle, from which we move into a new era of enlightenment. Those who learn how to live ethical lifestyles, of service to the Hierarchy, are fundamental to this momentous transition.

Some seek to serve as counselors, ministers or teachers. Regardless of vocation, if you learn to live consciously, in service to the planet and the Divine Plan, your life benefits the planet. Like a pebble dropped into a still pond, your intentions ripple out in subtle yet utterly powerful ways each day. Helping to heal and transform your community, your life becomes a ministry. Your place of work is like a temple. And you lead others by example.

All of this is the nature of spiritual leadership in the Aquarian Age. If you seek preparation to better serve in this way and would like to associate with others of like mind, here is an opportunity.

What the school offers—and why

Many have prophesied that mystery schools would reappear in the Aquarian Age. Their purpose is to train initiates in preparation for the externalization of the Hierarchy.

Sancta Sophia Seminary was established in 1978 to provide a one-of-a-kind, esoteric spiritual education. Five levels of off-campus and residential programs are offered. They provide deep understanding. As well, certification is earned by candidates who wish to become counselors, spiritual healing practitioners, ministers, or teachers of the Ageless Wisdom. In the Western world, the Ageless Wisdom is also called Esoteric Christianity.

The story behind the school and its founder

In 1980, Sancta Sophia's dean, Carol E. Parrish-Harra, was revealed to the greater public by author Ruth Montgomery, in the best-selling *Threshold to Tomorrow*. The book elaborated upon Carol's remarkable psychic and spiritual ability, and it described her role as a messenger in the new age.

Soon thereafter, Carol was guided by her Master to move the school from Florida to a place of greater safety during Earth changes and other tribulations. She was led to a specific, remote location in the beautiful Ozark Mountains of eastern Oklahoma to build Sancta Sophia.

Today, in addition to her personal teaching of Sancta Sophia students, Carol oversees all seminary classes and advisors. And she continues to minister, publish widely acclaimed books and audiocassette programs; she is a sought-after international speaker.

Spiritually charged location enhances growth

The magnificent, wooded, 400-acre mountain top setting where Carol was guided to build Sancta Sophia is also the home of the respected intentional community, Sparrow Hawk Village.

The village is a harmonious environment of 50 homes, office buildings and church. It has lovely gardens, good drinking water and a sophisticated infrastructure. Villagers are self-supporting people who live, learn, meditate and worship together.

Most important, the church sanctuary is centered on a vortex of special energies created by a star-shaped convergence of Earth ley lines. This creates a unique enclosure of spiritual energies which enhances the synergy of living, learning and personal growth for every Sancta Sophia student. The village is a sacred space which helps those who visit to heal and make their lives whole. The spiritual vortex creates an environment for the training of initiates and preparation for the externalization of the Hierarchy.

How the program creates personal transformation

Whether an off-campus or a residential program is chosen, the emphasis behind every student's program is the unique, transformational process guided by master teacher, Dean Carol E. Parrish-Harra.

The process is synergistic. It starts with a format of meaningful home study and meditation techniques tailored to your personal goals. Month by month an individually assigned advisor acts as your spiritual mentor, using telephone sessions or in-person meetings or communicating by mail. Then the entire process is catalyzed during periodic class weeks as you visit and enjoy the spiritually charged atmosphere at Sparrow Hawk Village. In fact, *Gateway of Liberation* is a required text in the Sancta Sophia course, "Training of the Initiate."

Five levels of certification available

The distinctive process of home study, meditation, spiritual mentoring and periodic classes at the village prepares the student to serve the Divine Plan and the planet in one of five ways.

First, Practitioners gain legal certification to serve as well-prepared lay ministers in counseling, spiritual healing or teaching. Second, Teachers of Esoteric Philosophy are educators for the new paradigms of spirituality now emerging on the planet. Third, Ordination prepares ministers in Esoteric Christianity to bring the true Ageless Wisdom into metaphysical and mainstream churches of the world. Ordinations are endorsed by the International Council of Community Churches. Membership in this post-denominational, ecumenical Christian organization assists our ministers to bridge effectively to mainstream, exoteric Christianity.

Additionally, two other levels of certification are available to a limited enrollment in the graduate school. For students with the requisite background, commitment and high creativity, Carol assists in designing programs leading to one of several Master's or Doctoral Degrees.

All programs are very reasonable in cost.

How to get more information

Do you seek to serve as a spiritual healing practitioner, minister, counselor, or teacher? If so, Sancta Sophia programs can prepare you to participate in the work of the Hierarchy as a spiritually awakened leader as we enter the modern era of enlightenment.

If you are interested in more information, you are invited to call the Registrar at (918) 456-3421, or write to Sancta Sophia Seminary, 11 Summit Ridge Drive–Dept.1, Tahlequah, OK 74464. If you wish, request the name of the affiliated center, church or class nearest you. Or, send in the order form at the end of this book.

"This book is a must for anyone doing dreamwork."

Richard Grams
The Leading Edge Review

"Among the many books which offer insight into the meaning of dream symbols, I find Ms. Tanner's to be the most approachable and useful, especially for beginning and intermediate explorers on this path."

H. Roberta Ossana, editor
Dream Network Journal

THE MYSTICAL, MAGICAL, MARVELOUS WORLD OF DREAMS

Wilda B. Tanner

Here is a proven method for using dreams to heal, solve problems and attain guidance for health, wealth, happiness and understanding. This bestseller, now in its 6th printing, is written for the spiritual seeker from a philosophical perspective.

In the first section of her mystical, magical, marvelous book, Wilda explains such phenomena as lucid dreaming, ESP or precognitive dreams, death-and-dying dreams, past-life dreams and nightmares. She also offers valuable insights on how to recall, interpret and work with dream symbols. The second section of this comprehensive book features a 260-page glossary of dream symbols and interpretations, plus an extensive cross-referenced index.

Wilda's joy and enthusiasm are contagious and her teachings, while deeply meaningful, are couched in simple language suited to every age.

Wilda B. Tanner has taught dream interpretation throughout the Unite States and Canada and has also been a frequent radio and T.V. guest. She is an ordained minister, teacher and philosopher.

$14.95 / tradepaper / 380pp / ISBN 0-945027-02-8

• **To purchase this book, please use the enclosed order form** •

"What Joseph Campbell has done with myth and ritual at the cognitive level, Carol Parrish-Harra does at the practical level. This work is a milestone and a 'must' for any person wishing to understand the deeper psycho-spiritual aspects of the complex human personality."

THE BOOK OF RITUALS
Personal and Planetary Transformation

Rev. Carol Parrish-Harra

You will benefit from the author's vast knowledge of astrology as you read about your specific sun sign and the "celestial hierarchy" associated with it. The author explains the exact challenges you face on your spiritual path and gives practical advice on how to open your physical and non-physical senses to effectively utilize the many subtle energies of the universe.

This highly original work presents specific rituals involving prayer, song, chanting, dance and meditation for each full moon period and for major festivals.

Reverend Carol Parrish-Harra, author of dozens of books and teaching tapes, has been identified by Ruth Montgomery as an Aquarian Age messenger. She is Dean of Sancta Sophia Seminary, founder and pastor of the Light of Christ Community Church and cofounder of Sparrow Hawk Village, an intentional spiritual community in Tahlequah, OK.

$14.95 / tradepaper / 280pp / ISBN 0-945027-10-9

• TO ORDER, PLEASE SEE THE LAST PAGE OF THIS SECTION •

"A beautifully written book that understands death and dying from the holistic perspective of the New Age. It deserves a wide audience; I highly recommend it."

Dr. Kenneth Ring, Director
International Association for Near-Death Studies
Author, *Life After Death, Heading Towards Omega*

THE NEW AGE HANDBOOK ON DEATH AND DYING

Rev. Carol Parrish-Harra

Proven techniques for expanding and transforming painful views of death are offered in this profound book of life-affirming wisdom. These insights have evolved out of the author's ministries with terminally ill patients and their families, from her own near-death experience and from her grief following the sudden loss of her daughter and granddaughter.

Counselors, family members and friends alike will find this book to be an excellent source of guidance and comfort in helping others prepare for the death experience. Join with Reverend Parrish-Harra as she seeks to facilitate a better understanding of spiritual teachings concerned with death and affirm a stronger belief in a living Creator with a perfect plan.

"...helps guide our hearts towards healing resolutions...shines a light on grief, convincing us we can face death, and learn and grow in the process."

BettyClare Moffatt, author
Cofounder, Mothers of AIDS Patients

$9.95 / tradepaper / 196pp / ISBN 0-945027-09-5

• TO ORDER, PLEASE USE THE FORM WHICH FOLLOWS •

"A great book for beginners,
Doe has made bite-size pieces out of com-
plex theory. Best of all, an astrology book
that isn't intimidating!"

Carol E. Parrish-Harra, Ph.D.
Best-selling author and spiritual teacher
Dean, Sancta Sophia Seminary

DO YOU SPEAK ASTROLOGY?
Learn the Language of the Skies

Doe Donovan

This book will prove especially valuable to those just beginning to learn to speak "the language of the skies." Doe's lively conversational writing style shortens potentially lengthy explanations as she describes signs, planets and aspects. Her interpretations are fascinating and include the natal charts of many famous personalities, such as Johnny Carson, Marilyn Monroe, Madonna, Michael Jordan and General Norman Schwarzkopf.

Doe Donovan's extraordinary presentation of traditional astrology has generated a distinct and lucid teaching book. She has simplified the complex study of astrology in a great how-to manner, using a contemporary approach to a centuries-old subject.

Doe Donovan is a professional astrologer and has been a faculty member at the American Federation of Astrologers biennial conventions. She is also a frequent contributor for the AFA Journal. Her background includes ten years of teaching communications arts and graduate work in education.

$12.95 / tradepaper / 272pp / ISBN 0-945027-05-2

• TO ORDER THIS BOOK, PLEASE USE THE ENCLOSED FORM •

AUDIO TAPES FOR YOUR GROWTH
by Carol E. Parrish-Harra, Ph.D.

ADVENTURE IN AWARENESS
Spiritual students seeking a greater understanding of esoteric concepts will find this series of 36 teaching lectures to be an invaluable resource. Carol presents a thorough exploration of Ageless Wisdom concepts including many tools and techniques to facilitate your spiritual growth.

    SERIES I - Breadth of Esoteric Teachings
    SERIES II - Awakening Our Inner Consciousness
    SERIES III - Toward Deeper Self-Realization

$60 per series. Each contains twelve 90-minute cassettes in clear plastic case

MEDITATION PLUS
Spiritual students will move toward an increasing awareness of the divinity within and greater expression of balance, joy and creativity through a variety of meditation techniques. Each tape side is a complete exercise designed to encourage the self-unfoldment of the inner nature.
$30 - six 45-minute cassettes in album case

COMING TO THE SUNRISE
These advanced meditation techniques guide the serious student to greater progress in self-purification. Mandalas from the book *Energy Ecstacy* by Bernard Gunther are used in the visualization portion of each exercise. Recommended for advanced students only.
$25 - four 60-minute cassettes in album case
$12.95 - *Energy Ecstacy* by Bernard Gunther

HEALING
A variety of healing methods to help students discover their own techniques for working with and understanding healing energy are explored. The amazing discovery of healing energy flowing through us opens the door to a new reality as we begin to *know* of this energy's existence and desire to use it in service to others.
$30 - six 45-minute cassettes in album case

NEW AGE CHRISTIANITY
Each of us, as New Age Christians, can discover the Christ-Within through expansion of consciousness. With fixed intent, we can grasp the Truths revealed by the Christ and use them to change our lives and our world.
$30 - six 60-minute cassettes in album case

EXPERIENCE NEW DIMENSIONS
Psychic skills gradually deliver us to our soul level of work and also to new realizations of ourselves as spiritual and divine beings. Carol presents this series of exercises to teach and encourage the exploration of psychic development.
$35 - six 60-minute cassettes in album case

THE AQUARIAN ROSARY
These beautiful prayers are intended to stimulate the mind and heart to a greater utilization of the Lots Of Vital Energies (LOVE) of the unfolding human soul. Carol provides an introduction to the Aquarian Rosary plus recordings of the Joyful, Sorrowful and Glorious Mysteries. Designed for use with her book of the same title.
$12.95 - two 60-minute cassettes in album case
$8.95 - *The Aquarian Rosary* (book)

• TO ORDER THESE TAPES, PLEASE USE THE ENCLOSED FORM •